IRREGULAR
WARFARE

THE FUTURE
MILITARY STRATEGY
FOR SMALL STATES

SANDOR FABIAN

ISBN:150849052X
ISBN-13:9781508490524

This book is dedicated to those strategic thinkers
who are ready to think without the box.

CONTENTS

ACKNOWLEDGMENTS

Since my commission as an officer, I have had the privilege of working with remarkable colleagues. Five of them, Major Attila Krezinger, Lieutenant Colonel Gabor Santa, Lieutenant Colonel Norbert Tajti, Lieutenant Colonel Sandor Gyenge, and Colonel Imre Porkolab, became not only my mentors, but my close friends. Their professionalism and leadership have had a great effect on my professional improvement, and through that, an enormous influence on this thesis. I am deeply grateful to them for their outstanding support.

I owe many thanks to the faculty of the Naval Postgraduate School, Department of Defense Analysis, for sharing their amazing knowledge and experience with me and opening my mind to an entirely new way of thinking. Special thanks go to my second reader, Lieutenant Colonel Michael Richardson, whose initial guidance and in-process critiques helped me keep my research on track.

My greatest gratitude goes to my advisor, John Arquilla, for honoring me with his precious time and erudition. More than any of my previous professors, instead of teaching me what to think, he taught me how to think. By opening my eyes to the importance of harvesting from the edge, Professor Arquilla has led me into a new world, which I deeply appreciate.

My wife, Beatrix, and daughter, Bibor Hanga, have been the single most important source of support of me for the past eighteen months. Without their dedication and love, this work would have never been completed.

CHAPTER 1
INTRODUCTION

A. BACKGROUND

During the Cold War, deterrence was based on the conventional military power of the two large alliances and their offsetting nuclear capabilities. Their example provided a baseline for small nations to think about their own self-defense. The fall of the Soviet Union changed the longstanding polarized world order, and the emergence of new international and local powers has changed the way certain countries look at the issue of self-defense now. No doubt the central concept of defensive action remains the ability to deter future enemies from aggression. The theory of deterrence has been a focus of researchers for decades. Thomas Schelling, for example, explains that "there is a difference between taking what you want and making someone give it to you, between fending off assault and making someone afraid to assault you, between holding what people are trying to take and making them afraid to take it, between losing what someone can forcibly take and giving it up to avoid risk or damage. It is the difference between defense and deterrence."[1] Schelling's deterrence theory is based in a state's diplomacy and military-strategy development. He argues that in the development of a state's military strategy—its capacity to hurt its enemy—lies a key motivating element in deterring its adversaries and avoiding conflict. To successfully deter another state, the use of force must be anticipated, but should be avoidable by means of compliance. In Schelling's view, the foundation of successful deterrence is the use of power to inflict damage as bargaining power, to influence another party's behavior.[2] Paul K. Huth explains it similarly when he states that deterrence is the application of threats by one side in order to convince the other side to abandon its intention of initiating some type of action.[3] Lawrence Freedman

---

[1] Thomas C. Schelling, *Arms and Influence*, (New Haven: Yale University Press, 1966), 2.

[2] Schelling, *Arms and Influence*, 1-20.

[3] Paul K. Huth, "Deterrence and International Conflict: Empirical Findings and Theoretical Debate," *Annual Review of Political Science* 2 (1999): 25-48.

categorizes deterrence as punishment and denial. According to him, the essence of punishment is the manipulation of the "behavior of others through conditional threats,"[4] while denial is the implementation of guerrilla strategy.[5] However, while the theory of how to deter an enemy looks well established, the question of what happens if the threats are not enough and an actual "aggression phase" starts is not well explored.

History suggests that small nation–states have four general choices, based on their geographical location, available natural resources, and foreign-policy goals, to sustain effective deterrence and defensive capabilities. First, they may try to provide their own security by imitating the military power of larger states through sustainment of a traditional military force (army, air force, navy, etc.). But many of these small nations are struggling with financial issues and have limited resources to allocate for the sustainment of a large

---

[4] Lawrence Freedman, *Deterrence,* (New York: Polity Press, 2004), 6.

[5] Freedman, *Deterrence,* 14-17.

military. They live under the illusion of having a capable defense force, but when it comes to a test, the results can be very painful.[6] Second, small countries with restricted military capability may join an alliance and rely on the collective-security notion of defense. As history shows, alliances have always struggled with the issue of "entrapment" and "abandonment." In some cases, when it has come to actual aggression, no doubt alliances have worked; but in other cases, they have failed miserably.[7]

Third, small nations can adopt neutrality as a solution for homeland defense. Although neutrality might allow the country to retain its sovereignty, it

---

[6] The Georgian-Russian conflict in 2008 is an example of how a small nation that had tried to imitate big ones failed against a larger enemy.

[7] The invasion of Poland in September 1939 by Germany and a few weeks later, Russia is an example of alliance failure. On the 25th of August, Poland signed the Polish-British Common Defense Pact as an annex to the already existing Franco-Polish Military Alliance. In those France and Great Britain committed themselves to the defense of Poland, guaranteeing to preserve Polish independence. The invasion of Poland led Britain and France to declare war on Germany on 3 September. However, they did little to affect the outcome of the September campaign. This lack of direct help led many Poles to believe that they had been betrayed by their Western allies.

has always been a sensitive issue, since it can work only if it is accepted by the potential aggressor as well. Finally, small countries can try to obtain weapons of mass destruction. Since many small nations have signed nonproliferation treaties, even a sign of the intention to obtain WMDs can cause very serious international-relations problems, not only politically, but economically as well. The other disadvantage of a nuclear-deterrence-based self-defense strategy is that, when it fails, the country has to have the will to use WMDs against the aggressor to have any real meaning.[8]

All the above-mentioned ideas are based on traditional ways of thinking about war and defending a country, but a detailed analysis of history provides other possibilities worth considering. For example, history shows that irregular strategies have been successful quite a few times when a small force faced a much bigger and stronger enemy. Recent history, as in Vietnam,

---

[8] The Democratic People's Republic of Korea provides an example of successful WMD acquisition as enhancing security and defense capability.

Chechnya, Lebanon, Iraq, and Afghanistan, teaches us again the painful lessons of fighting against irregulars. Countries with a traditional, orthodox military mindset and organizations have spent the last couple of decades trying to figure out the weaknesses of irregulars and how to fight against them effectively. However, the other side of the coin has been poorly explored. What can be learned and used from the strength of irregular strategies? Can an irregular-warfare strategy be incorporated into the homeland defense of smaller nations?

1. Research Question

How should small countries defend themselves?

2. Implied Research Question

What is a possible alternative method for defense for small nations beyond the above-mentioned four traditional models?

3. Hypotheses

1. During an invasion of its territory, a small state has a better chance to defeat a numerically and

technologically superior enemy when utilizing irregular-warfare techniques instead of traditional military approaches.

2. Irregular-warfare strategy is more effective when the irregular defense force contains and is led by professional military members.

3. Irregular-warfare strategy is more effective when the irregular defense force is organized, trained, and equipped for irregular war before the conflict, rather than when it arises ad hoc, in the wake of conventional defeat.

B. RESEARCH DESIGN

In 1975, the American Army Colonel Harry Summers traveled to Hanoi as a member of a negotiating party. He got into a conversation with a

North Vietnamese colonel named Tu, and told him that the North Vietnamese forces had never defeated the American troops on the battlefield. The North Vietnamese colonel responded: "That may be so, but it is also irrelevant."[9] The main goal of this thesis is to analyze the theory that is it possible to use irregular warfare as a national military strategy and to adopt a "professional, irregular defense force" concept as a country's homeland-defense force; and, if these are indeed valid possibilities, to explore the conditions under which they are preferable to conventional defense.

It is not the goal of this research to identify single countries as possible subjects of the theory or to provide a general framework for how to organize, train, equip, or sustain a professional, irregular defense force. It is also beyond the scope of this investigation to determine whether it is cheaper to sustain an irregular-type military organization than a conventional force, but the likelihood is that an irregular force will cost much less. If the theory is

---

[9] Harry G. Summers Jr., *On Strategy: a Critical Analysis of the Vietnam War*, (Novato: Presidio Press, 1982), 1.

proven valid, these questions should become the subject of further research.

The first part of this thesis will clarify the definition of small states to establish a conceptual basis for analyzing the four defense possibilities noted above. The basic assumption of this research is that the assessment of the traditional ways of defense will present an opportunity for a different, more self-reliant approach to provide small countries with their own defenses. To try to fill this gap, this thesis will introduce and investigate the "professional, irregular defense force" theory as a possible homeland-defense solution. The second part of this project will focus on historical case studies, in which state and non-state actors (and their military or paramilitary forces) either combined regular with irregular warfare or abandoned conventional operations altogether, using only irregular warfare to engage their enemies. Analyzing and assessing both successful and failed cases will help identify the key conditions under which the suggested irregular warfare approach is preferable to conventional warfare. The final part of this thesis will summarize findings and, based on the results, will support or deny the validity and exportability of the proffered theory on irregular warfare strategy and the "professional" force that might wage such conflicts.

C. RESEARCH METHOLODGY

To explore the concept of a professional, irregular defense force and related strategies, this thesis will present six historical case studies and provide a detailed analysis of each, focusing on the side that used irregular warfare. To narrow the scope of the investigation, this thesis will analyze historical cases when military or paramilitary forces defending a homeland either combined conventional strategy with irregular warfare techniques or avoided the conventional, orthodox way of waging war and conducted irregular warfare only, against a numerically and technologically superior conventional enemy. To test the hypothesis effectively, this research will introduce longitudinal and cross-sectional analysis of successful and failed historical cases.

First, this thesis will introduce two cases with similar backgrounds: former colonies fighting for freedom and independence against a major empire. Both colonies started the conflict without a previously existing conventional military force, while their enemies possessed large and technologically superior military capabilities. In these cases, the weak side had to rely on irregular, militia-type forces at the beginning of the conflict to gain time for building a conventional defense force. These irregular forces continued to play a key role during the entire conflict, even after a conventional military was established. The first two cases will consist of the American Revolutionary War, which will be presented as a successful case, and the Second Boer War, an example of failure. These cases will investigate why certain characteristics led to success in one case and failure in the other.

To further investigate those conditions, a third case study will focus on the events of the First

World War in German East Africa. In this case, an already existing, conventionally organized and trained, colonial-defense force, after realizing that conventional defense held no chance of success against an inexhaustible enemy, waged an entire war by following irregular strategy. The fourth case study analyzes the operations of the Yugoslav partisans during the Second World War. In this case, a small state, with its conventional military forces defeated and territories occupied, organized guerrilla forces on an ad-hoc basis and launched an irregular campaign to engage the occupying military.

Finally, two contemporary cases challenge the validity of the hypotheses and exportability of the proposed homeland-defense strategy. The First Russo–Chechen War and the Second Lebanese War are useful examples how the use of ancient and modern elements of irregular warfare can dramatically increase the weaker side's chance of defeating a conventional adversary. In all cases studies, this research will employ at least three different sources to confirm findings and make sure sources agree.

To identify the common fundamentals and characteristics of the case studies and help in their analysis and assessment, it is important to establish a research model. Since the basic pillar of the proposed irregular-warfare strategy is guerrilla warfare, this research will use a model that adopts the principles of the most significant irregular- and guerrilla-warfare theorists, including Carl von Clausewitz, Mao Zedong, Ernesto "Che" Guevara, and General Vo Nguyen Giap. A summary explanation of their warfighting principles is necessary before moving on to a detailed description of the research model.

The first contributor is Carl von Clausewitz. It might be surprising that this thesis considers him a significant irregular-warfare theorist, since his name is identified with the definitions of conventional war as "a continuation of policy by other means,"[10] and of war in general as "the

---

[10] Carl von Clausewitz, *On War*, (Princeton: Princeton

application of armed forces by a state to destroy the enemy army to compel another state to follow the attacker's will."[11] Many scholars dispute his relevance in studying the dynamics of today's irregular conflicts. For example, Martin van Creveld, supported by Edward Luttwak and Steven Metz, states that because low-intensity conflicts are today's primary way of war, Clausewitz's ideas are no longer valid, or possibly wrong.[12] On the other hand, several researchers, including Werner Hahlweg and Christopher Daase, have gone beyond Clausewitz's famous book, *On War*, and, by analysis of his other works such as "Lectures on Small War," given at the Allgemeine Kriegsschule in c. 1811, and "Bekenntnisdenkschrift" ("Memorandum of Confession") of 1812, find that Clausewitz studied guerrilla warfare and its principles extensively.[13]

University Press, 1976), 210.

[11] Hew Strachan, and Andreas Herberg-Rothe, *Clausewitz in the Twenty First Century*, (Oxford: Oxford University Press, 2007), 186.

[12] Martin Van Creveld , *The Transformation of War*, (New York: The Free Press, 1991), ix.

Clausewitz's guerrilla-warfare theory was based on his analysis of the rebellion in the Vendée between 1793 and 1796, the Tyrolean conflict of 1809, and the Spanish guerrilla war against the French from 1808 to 1814.[14] He was also influenced by Scharnhorst and Gneisenau's *Landsturm* idea, which proposed "the establishment of a national militia in Prussia"[15] to "hinder the enemy's advance and bar his retreat, to keep him continually on the move, to capture his ammunition, food, supplies, couriers and recruits, to seize his hospitals, and to attack him by night, in short, harassing, tormenting, tiring and destroying him either individually or his units wherever possible."[16] Based on these influences and his case studies, Clausewitz's theory of "small war" evolved over

---

[13] Strachan and Herberg-Rothe, *Clausewitz in the Twenty First Century*, 183.

[14] Werner Hahlweg, "Clausewitz and Guerrilla Warfare," *Journal of Strategic Studies* 9 (1986): 127.

[15] Walter Laqueur, *Guerrilla Warfare. A Historical and Critical Study*, (New Brunswick: Transaction Publishers, 1998), 112.

[16] Laqueur, *Guerrilla Warfare*, 112.

time. During his initial lectures, addressing the lieutenants and captains of the Prussian army,[17] he considered guerrilla operations as a "specific form of military operation by small units to reconnoiter the enemy's positions and harass his lines of communication"[18] and did not consider them an independent form of war. However, in the "Bekenntnisdenkschrift," he changed his view. Experiencing the superior power of France and the weakness of the conventional Prussian army, he saw small war in a revolutionary way. Clausewitz considered the mobilization of the masses and irregular warfare as a crucial element of war with the aim "to harass and exhaust the enemy's army in order to change his policy. Small war gained a rather distinct form in Clausewitz's thinking."[19] He suggested such a war to liberate Prussia from Napoleon's army in 1812. He concluded that

---

[17] Laqueur, *Guerrilla Warfare*, 110.

[18] Strachan and Herberg-Rothe, *Clausewitz in the Twenty First Century*, 187.

[19] Strachan and Herberg-Rothe, *Clausewitz in the Twenty First Century*, 187.

Prussia was too weak and could not fight the French in open battle. "The alternative, however, should neither be surrender nor an unholy alliance with France, but the strongest possible defense through a Spanish civil war in Germany."[20] In developing his theory of small wars, Clausewitz identified several key principles of guerrilla warfare that are useful in this thesis' research model.

According to Clausewitz, during small war, the guerrillas, who should fight "by units of between twenty and four-hundred men,"[21] are normally facing a superior enemy whom they must avoid to make their forces last. He states that the crucial element of small war as a defensive strategy is time, which works against the occupying army while not affecting, or affecting to a smaller extent, the defender.[22] Small wars, waged by a population in its own country, can be fought for a long time.

---

[20] Strachan and Herberg-Rothe, *Clausewitz in the Twenty First Century*, 190.

[21] Laqueur, *Guerrilla Warfare*, 110.

[22] Strachan and Herberg-Rothe, *Clausewitz in the Twenty First Century*, 190.

Thus, for the occupying force and the defending party, different criteria apply for success. Clausewitz stated that the way a small war is fought differs greatly from large conventional battles, since they require more "courage and temerity but also demanded the utmost caution."[23]

Clausewitz lists several conditions that can enhance the effectiveness of guerrillas. First, he suggests that defensive war be waged within a country's own territory. "The greater the surface area of the country the greater will be the contact with enemy forces, and, thus, the greater the potential effect of a guerrilla war. This could, in time, destroy the basic foundations of the enemy forces"[24] Second, guerrillas must prevent the enemy from being able to deliver a single, decisive stroke. Clausewitz states that "resistance should never materialize as a concrete body, otherwise the enemy can direct sufficient force at its core, crush it, and take many prisoners,"[25] and if it happens,

---

[23] Laqueur, *Guerrilla Warfare*, 110.

[24] Hahlweg , "Clausewitz and Guerrilla Warfare," 131.

"the people will lose heart and, believing that the issue has been decided and further efforts would be useless, drop their weapons."[26] Fourth, "the national character must be suited to this type of armed confrontation."[27] Fifth, the terrain for operations must be rough and impassable, because of wilderness, swamps, and mountains. Although terrain is important, guerrillas should not turn to a fixed defense. They have to remain flexible and only defend certain features, including "points of access to a mountain area, or the dikes across a marsh, or points at which a river can be crossed, as long as this appears possible."[28] Finally, Clausewitz emphasized the importance of secrecy and the power of having informational advantage over the enemy.[29] These principles and conditions, and Clausewitz's "people's war" theory in general,

---

[25] Hahlweg, "Clausewitz and Guerrilla Warfare," 131.

[26] Hahlweg, "Clausewitz and Guerrilla Warfare," 132.

[27] Hahlweg, "Clausewitz and Guerrilla Warfare," 131.

[28] Hahlweg, "Clausewitz and Guerrilla Warfare," 132.

[29] Laqueur, *Guerrilla Warfare*, 110.

provide several key foundations for the research model used in this thesis.

The next contributor is Mao Zedong and his main work, *Yu Chi Chan (On Guerrilla Warfare)*. Mao provided important insights on the relationship of conventional and guerrilla forces, and the training, support, and operations of unconventional units. He introduced some key principles about guerrilla warfare that remain timeless. According to Mao, guerrilla operations are not independent from the conventional form of warfare, but a part of it. He explains the direct relationship between conventional and guerrilla forces by stating, "during the progress of hostilities, guerrillas gradually develop into orthodox forces that operate in conjunction with other units of the regular army."[30] Mao considers guerrilla warfare as "a weapon that a nation inferior in arms and military equipment may employ against a more powerful aggressor nation."[31]

---

[30] Mao Tse-tung, *On Guerrilla Warfare* translated by Samuel B. Griffith, (Urbana:University of Illinois Press, 2000), 42.

To explain his concept, Mao established some basic principles.

One of Mao's characteristics of guerrilla warfare was that it follows in three phases, which are sometimes barely distinguishable and many times overlap. The first phase of guerrilla warfare is the establishment and development of the organization. The next phase is the conduct of guerrilla operations, such as direct attacks on vulnerable military and police targets, sabotage, and assassinations. The third phase is the period for destroying the enemy. According to Mao, during this phase the guerrilla force transforms into a conventional, orthodox military and engages the enemy in conventional fighting. This part is important for this research, since the basic idea of this thesis advocates the opposite: keeping the force irregular through the entire conflict.

Another principle identified by Mao is the need for the cooperation and support of the population. This support is necessary to establish

---

[31] Mao, *On Guerrilla Warfare*, 42.

operational bases and to train, equip, and sustain guerrilla units. The other important characteristic in Mao's strategy is the ability to adapt. The guerrilla strategy "must be adjusted based on the enemy situation, the terrain, the existing lines of communication, the relative strengths, the weather, and the situation of the people."[32] Mao emphasizes that guerrilla units need decentralized control, due to their organization and tactics, but with close coordination with conventional forces. "In guerrilla strategy, the enemy's rear, flanks, and other vulnerable spots are his vital points, and there he must be harassed, attacked, dispersed, exhausted, and annihilated. Only in this way can guerrillas carry out their mission of independent guerrilla action and coordination with the effort of the regular armies."[33] Mao referred to organization as a fundamental characteristic. He explained that the origins of the guerrilla forces may stem from five roots: the "civilian" population, conventional

---

[32] Mao, *On Guerrilla Warfare*, 46.
[33] Mao, *On Guerrilla Warfare*, 46.

military units, local militias, turncoat enemy soldiers, and criminal groups. Mao also discusses the importance of equipment, emphasizing that guerrillas need light weapons and that there is no need for standardization. Equipping the guerrilla units must be a combined product of the population, the regular army, and the use of captured weapons.

Mao summarizes, "we must promote guerrilla warfare as a necessary strategical auxiliary to orthodox operations; we must neither assign it the primary position in our war strategy nor substitute it for mobile and positional warfare as conducted by orthodox forces."[34] This conclusion on guerrilla strategy will be an important part of this investigation and contributes significant points to the establishment of the research model.

The third key contributor is Ernesto "Che" Guevara and his book, *Guerrilla Warfare*, in which he introduces his theory about guerrilla warfare, called the "Foco." The basic element of Guevara's theory is small and mobile groups of guerrilla

---

[34] Mao, *On Guerrilla Warfare*, 57.

cadres, which travel around rural areas to ignite rebellion among the peasants against the ruling regime. These "fighter teachers" provide training and general leadership for locals in order to mobilize and launch guerrilla attacks from rural areas.[35] Guevara's theory agrees with Mao's on several questions. First, he emphasizes the importance of popular support for guerrilla forces. Second, Guevara explains that "the countryside is the basic area for armed fighting."[36] Third, he agrees that the guerrilla force has to be transformed into a conventional army to fulfill the overall goal, the destruction of the enemy. Fourth, Guevara emphasizes the ability to adapt to the conditions of the operational environment and adjust guerrilla tactics as the situation changes, in order to hold the initiative and the ability to surprise the enemy. Nevertheless, while Mao emphasizes the

---

[35] Gordon H. McCormick, (2011) *Seminar on Guerrilla Warfare,* DA Department, NPS.

[36] Joshua Johnson, "From Cuba to Bolivia: Guevara's Foco Theory in Practice," *Innovations: a Journal of Politics*, Volume 6 (2006): 27.

importance of prior establishment of the proper conditions for guerrilla war, Guevara states "it is not necessary to wait until all the conditions for making revolution exist; the insurrection can create them."[37] Guevara explains several other important factors of guerrilla warfare. He emphasizes the importance of knowing the terrain and thoroughly understanding guerrilla tactics. According to Guevara, guerrilla forces need a special strategy to achieve their goals while also preserving their units, calling for "the analysis of the objectives to be achieved in the light of the total military situation and the overall ways of reaching these objectives."[38] Guevara believed that special tactics characterize guerrilla warfare, especially mobility, sabotage, night operations, treatment of the civilian population, and any "practical methods of achieving the grand strategic objectives."[39] For example,

---

[37] Johnson, "From Cuba to Bolivia: Guevara's Foco Theory in Practice," 27.

[38] Ernesto Che Guevara, *Guerrilla Warfare*, (New York: Classic House Books, 2009), 10.

[39] Che Guevara, *Guerrilla Warfare*, 15.

"One of the weakest points of the enemy is transportation by road and railroad. It is virtually impossible to maintain a vigil yard by yard over a transport line, a road, or railroad."[40] Guerrilla operations have to focus on the enemy's lines of communications and its resupply system to effectively undermine conventional operations and inflict significant casualties.

The last strategist whose principles influenced this thesis's research model is General Vo Nguyen Giap and his book, *The Military Art of People's War*. General Giap was appointed commander of Viet Minh forces in 1945, when the Indochinese Communist Party decided to fight the Japanese and French forces in China. General Giap was not a pure Maoist; but he tested Mao's guerrilla strategy in combat situations during the early years of his command and analyzed the reasons behind Mao's successes and failures. Based on his experiences and observations, General Giap developed a new kind of guerrilla-strategy model.

---

[40] Che Guevara, *Guerrilla Warfare*, 15.

General Giap's "new guerrilla-warfare model" follows the main line of Mao's principles, but introduces the need for more will and the ability to switch back and forth between the different types of warfare. He modified Mao's principles to fit the time and space where a war is fought. Like Mao, General Giap divides guerrilla warfare into three phases, but with significant differences. The first phase is the "stage of contention," which covers the organization of the movement and the conduct of guerrilla-type operations. This period serves for building up the organization and limited guerrilla activity, to target the enemy's morale and start attrition. According to General Giap, during this phase, military operations are to be conducted only when success is guaranteed. The next phase is the "period of equilibrium," a combination of guerrilla operations and conventional mobile warfare. This period is designed to establish the balance between the two opposing forces, and for the conventional forces to exploit guerrilla successes by occupying and holding significant locations. General Giap's final phase is the "stage of counteroffensive," a combination of mobile and positional warfare, in which the switch from guerrilla war to conventional war is completed and large conventional forces dominate the fighting; however, guerrilla-type operations do not cease to exist. [41] General Giap emphasizes the use of conventional forces during a much earlier phase than Mao, but at the same time, sustains the guerrilla character during all three phases.

Another significant difference in General Giap's model is the suggestion of fighting simultaneously in both rural and urban areas and using positional warfare. According to Mao's theory, guerrillas have to avoid being pinned down and must retreat to base areas. As Mao explains, "the enemy advances, we retreat; the enemy camps, we harass; the enemy tires, we attack; the enemy retreats, we pursue."[42] On the other hand, General

---

[41] Vo Nguyen Giap, *The Military Art of People's War: Selected Writings of General Vo Nguyen Giap*, edited by Russel Stetler, (Monthly Review Press, 1970), 62.

[42] Giap, *The Military Art of People's War*, 46.

Giap suggested the use of positional defense in the cities. The introduction of significant geographical locations and the need to hold them is a significant change to Mao's theory.

In sum, one can observe that the three theorists cited above recognize several common principles and characteristics for guerrilla warfare. These principles are reflected in the research model of this thesis, which incorporates historical perspectives to help find contemporary relevance. The research model consists of five components: background, strategy, organization and leadership, internal factors, and external factors.

Background, as the first component of the model, indicates that a historical overview will be provided in every case study. This part of the assessment will establish the reader's basic situational awareness and provide the detailed information necessary to understand the assessment process. This component will introduce the road to the conflict, the opposing parties and their goals, the main events, and an overview of the outcome.

The second component of the research model is strategy: how irregular warfare was employed by the weaker party in a conflict. This component will answer questions such as, What were the strategic goals, and how did irregular warfare support those goals? Was irregular warfare integrated into a conventional strategy, or was it the only way for the smaller side to engage the enemy? Through these questions, this thesis intends to discover the strategic conditions under which irregular warfare is preferable to conventional strategy.

The third part of the research model is an assessment of organization and leadership. Through analysis of irregular unit's organization and operational structure, one can answer the question, What effects did organization have on the engagements and final results of the conflict? By introducing the focal irregular leaders and assessing their personal and professional capabilities, this component also will discover the viability and exportability of any profile for successful irregular operations.

Internal factors are the fourth part of the assessment model. This component will investigate the importance of the types of tactics, the level of training given to irregulars, and the role of intelligence, raising such questions as, Why are irregular tactics so effective? Why can the enemy not counter them easily? How do these tactics take away the enemy's numerical or weapons superiority? When and how are irregulars trained? What level of training is necessary to fight effectively? Do irregulars have an intelligence advantage over their enemies? If so, is it significant?

The last component of the model is external factors. This part will first analyze the role of physical terrain in certain conflicts. Did it favor any side, and how did it influence the war? Is there a certain physical terrain required to fight irregular warfare? This component of the model will also investigate the importance of the social terrain, or in other words, the role of the population. Is popular support always needed for irregular`s success? If so, to what level? This component will also explore the role of havens and redoubts in irregular warfare and the significance of the international environment. Was there any outside support available for the irregulars? How did the international situation influence the end results of the conflict?

The following investigation of the above-described components intends to discover, through historical cases, possible conditions under which a small state might consider changing its traditional, orthodox understanding of military defense and developing a new mindset using irregular warfare as the foundational idea for homeland defense.

CHAPTER 2
DEFINITION OF KEY TERMS

A. DEFINING THE SMALL STATE

To establish a well-supported basic framework for this research, it is necessary to examine the various definitions of "small states." Martin Wight, in his book *Power Politics,* explains that "the smallness we are talking about when we speak of small powers is smallness relative to the international society they belong to."[43] According to Hakan Wiberg, author of the *The Security of Small Nations: Challenges and Defences*, the definitions of small states can be absolute or relational.[44] In case of an absolute definition, Wiberg suggests that "indicators of 'size' are sought, such as population, area, GNP, military capability, etc., and attempts are then made to correlate other variables with the size indicators." [45] On the other

---

[43] Martin Wight, *Power Politics*, (Penguin Books Ltd, 1979), 61.

[44] Hakan Wiberg, "The Security of Small Nations: Challenges and Defences," *Journal of Peace Research,* volume 24, number 4 (1987): 339.

[45] Wiberg, "The Security of Small Nations," 339.

hand, Wiberg's relational definition asserts that "the essence of 'smallness' is either lack of influence on the environment or high sensitivity to the environment and lack of immunity against influences from it, or both."[46] In his book, *Alliances and Small Powers*, Robert Rothstein writes "a small power is a state that recognizes it cannot obtain security primarily by use of its own capabilities, and that it must rely fundamentally on the aid of other states, institutions, processes, or developments to do so; the small power's belief in its inability to rely on its own means must also be recognized by the other states involved in international politics."[47] Although all these definitions are valuable, Michael I. Handel's definition is most useful for the purposes of this research. He states that a small state "is a state which is unable to contend in war with the great powers on anything like equal terms."[48] This thesis

---

[46] Wiberg, "The Security of Small Nations," 339.

[47] Robert L. Rothstein, *Alliances and Small Powers*, (Columbia University Press, 1968), 29.

[48] Michael I. Handel, *Weak States in the International*

will use this definition in answering the question, How should small states defend themselves?

The notion of smallness is always relative in a conflict, and depends on the situation—and can change in the aftermath of a particular conflict. The United States was a small state when it fought the Revolutionary War against the British Empire, but was generally the bigger power in many following wars. Germany was the major power at the beginning of the Second World War, but became a small state in the wake of its defeat. Iraq was a regional power when it occupied Kuwait in 1990, but became a small state afterward and again in 2003 when the US and its allies attacked. Smallness can be applied to any country that faces a numerically bigger, better equipped and trained, more effectively organized military force than its own.

B. TRADITIONAL DEFENSE STRATEGIES

Every state has to tailor its defense

System, (Gainsborough: Frank Cass and Co Ltd, 1990), 36.

capabilities to its national interests and the possible adversaries it may face in future conflicts. Every state's paramount national goal is to survive.[49] The best way to survive is to stay out of conflicts. In general, every state tries to avoid hostilities by creating some type of deterrence capability, which, in different shapes or forms, threatens an adversary with out-of-proportion losses in case of attack.[50] Every deterrence strategy is closely linked to a state's actual ability to defend itself, since after the possible failure of the deterrence phase, the state has to exercise the capability on which its deterrence was based.

States have historically tried to build their homeland-defense capabilities around four major strategies: imitating a major power's military capability; joining an alliance; assuming neutrality; or acquiring weapons of mass destruction. To

---

[49] Wiberg, "The Security of Small Nations," 340.

[50] Michael Richardson (2011) *Course lectures on Deterrence, Coercion and Crisis Management,* DA Department, NPS.

discover the advantages and disadvantages of these defense strategies and form a possible new way of thinking about homeland defense, it is necessary to assess these methods.

1. Imitating Major Powers

The first traditional way to approach homeland defense is to imitate a major power's military capabilities. The basic question is always, from whom does a state want to defend itself—for in the contemporary world, the list of possible adversaries can change quickly, and every state needs a solution that can be applied against the widest range of possible foes. Small states usually try to imitate in two ways. First, they sustain a relatively large military force with multiple services, including army, air force, navy, and in some cases Marine corps, in order to match their possible adversaries. In many cases, the cost of this approach is so high that their equipment is unavoidably old and obsolete. This strategy is based on the idea that a large number of troops and weapons might possibly compensate for the adversary's more sophisticated weapons. One of the major disadvantages of this approach is that a large number of troops and the resource requirements for maintaining old weapons systems can be a devastating financial challenge for small states in peacetime. Moreover, the probable effectiveness of the military force during a conflict is highly questionable.[51] History shows many catastrophic failures due to belief in this approach. In 1939, Poland, which had an army of close to a million and based its defensive strategy on a large number of mobile cavalry brigades, was defeated within a month by mechanized German forces and Soviet troops who joined in the attack.[52] During the Six-Day War, in 1967, Israel destroyed the entire Egyptian air force within two hours.[53] During the

---

[51] The Russo-Georgian conflict in 2008 is an example of how a small nation that had tried to imitate the military of a large state failed against an even larger enemy.

[52] Stanley S. Seidner, *Marshal Edward Śmigły-Rydz and the Defense of Poland*, (New York: Michigan University Press, 1978), 135-138.

[53] Lawrence Wright, *The Looming Tower: Al-Qaeda and the Road to 9/11*, (New York: Vintage Books, 2006), 45.

Russo–Georgian War, in 2008, "Georgia's army fled ahead of the Russian army's advance, turning its back and leaving Georgian civilians in the enemy's path. Its planes did not fly after the first few hours of contact. Its navy was sunk in the harbor, and its patrol boats were hauled away by Russian trucks on trailers."[54]

The other way for small states to try to imitate larger states' military capabilities is to sustain a significant military force with old weapon systems while, at the same time, getting into the competition of military research and development. The gap between the small and the large states in new weaponry has widened recently, to the disadvantage of the small states.[55] The resource requirements and costs of new major military systems have reached a level where even major states have serious issues in developing and sustaining them.[56]

---

[54] C. J. Chivers, and Thom Shanker, "Georgia Eager to Rebuild its Defeated Armed Forces" The New York Times. 03, September, 2008, accessed October 03, 2011, http://www.nytimes.com/2008/09/03/world/europe/03georgia.html?pagewanted=print.

[55] Wiberg, "The Security of Small Nations," 350.

Thus it has become "more and more hopeless for small states to try to 'keep up' by developing similar systems for themselves."[57] Of course, another solution comes to mind: namely, to procure these modern systems from the major states. This solution favors big states, but creates many disadvantages for the small states. One of these is the increased dependence on the major power and its will, especially during conflict, to resupply necessary "software updates" and other vital components, including spare parts and ammunition. The procurement solution does not serve small states' interests, since they should instead create more self-reliance to be able to provide their own defense.[58] The disadvantages of imitation usually inspire decision makers to look for alternative solutions. Another potential solution is to join an alliance.

---

[56] Wiberg, "The Security of Small Nations," 350.

[57] Wiberg, "The Security of Small Nations," 350.

[58] Wiberg, "The Security of Small Nations," 350.

2. Joining Alliances

Some states that either realizes that they cannot sustain a large military force, or just believe that their military capabilities are not enough to provide the desired level of security, seek to join an alliance as an alternative solution. According to security expert Heinz Gaertner, "Alliances can be defined as formal associations of states bound by the mutual commitment to use military force against non-member states to defend member states' integrity."[59] When joining an alliance, small states are looking for extended deterrent effects, increased military capability, and, in a multilateral alliance, less dependence on a single power. Scholars agree there are two basic ways to seek alliances. As Stephen Walt notes, "When confronted by a significant external threat, states may either balance or bandwagon. Balancing is defined as allying with others against the prevailing threat: bandwagoning refers to alignment with the source of danger."[60]

[59] Erich Reiter and Heinz Gaertner, *Small States and Alliance,* (Vienna: Physica-Verlag, 2001), 3.

[60] Stephen Walt, *The Origins of Alliances,* (Ithaca:

To do so, small states may establish a bilateral alliance with another small state or a major power, or may join a multilateral alliance.

Bilateral alliances are usually based on regional threats rather than global ones. Small states seek a more powerful ally to enhance their capabilities to defend against these regional threats. This approach carries two major disadvantages. First, small states must rely on a single ally to come to their aid when the need arises. An example of a successful bilateral alliance is the Mutual Defense Treaty between the United States and South Korea, signed in 1953 as a direct result of the Korean War. "The Mutual Defense Treaty is an institutional guarantee for the USFK to be stationed in Korea to deter another war on the Korean peninsula, and a legal ground for the Combined Defense System. It also serves as the foundation for other affiliated security arrangements and military agreements between the ROK and US governments and militaries."[61] On the other hand,

Cornell University Press, 1987), 17.

[61] The ROK-US Mutual Defense Treaty,

the Franco–Polish Kasprzycki–Gamelin Convention,[62] signed May 19, 1939, is an example of a complete failure. The second disadvantage of a bilateral alliance is the risk of the small state's being drawn into its partner's conflicts. This danger is called "entrapment" and usually requires an out-of-proportion effort from the small countries, as compared to their gains from the alliance.

Multilateral alliances are more favorable for small states than bilateral, because the multiple members of these alliances carry more deterrent power, greater defensive capability, and less dependence on a single state. On the other hand, these alliances, because of the many different interests involved, are hard to achieve and sustain as a functioning system. NATO, the world's largest

---

http://www.koreaembassyusa.org/bilateral/military/eng_milita ry4.asp, accessed 01 November, 2011.

[62] The alliance required both countries to intervene militarily in case of a German attack. The French even promised to launch an attack against Germany within three weeks in case of an offensive action against Poland.

Nicole Jordan, The *Popular Front and Central Europe. The Dilemmas of French Impotence 1918-1940*, (New York: Cambridge University Press, 1992), 294.

and most powerful military alliance, struggles to make decisions to take actions, because in many cases its members cannot agree on the proper level of response, or in some cases, even on the existence of a conflict. The disadvantages of bilateral alliances are also still present. However strongly multilateral alliances may require members to use military force in case of aggression against a member, nothing guarantees that the other members will perceive the threat to a small state as worthy of collective military action, and it is possible that the small state will be abandoned. This possibility is even greater when a conflict arises between two member states; the conflict between Turkey and Greece over Cyprus in 1974[63] is an example of the

---

[63] Following a Greek military coup in July 1974, Turkey sent invading forces as part of "Operation Attila" to protect the Turkish Cypriots and to guarantee the independence of Cyprus. The conflict ended with a cease fire agreement, which divided Cyprus into Turkish and Greek parts.

Kassimeris, Christos. "Greek Response to the Cyprus Invasion," *Small Wars and Insurgencies*, volume 19, number 2 (2008): 256–273, accessed November 01, 2011, http://www.tandfonline.com/doi/abs/10.1080/095923108020206 1398?journalCode=fswi20#preview, accessed 01 November, 2011.

weakness of multilateral alliances. The other disadvantage is the increased chance for being "entrapped," being "obligated to participate in a conflict in which they had no direct interest."[64] As history was shown, many times, "Alliances turn small wars into big wars."[65] The more small states depend on the alliance, the higher the risk of being dragged into another's conflicts. And the less the dependency among members, the higher the risk of mutual abandonment is during a war. To mitigate the risk of these disadvantages, small states can choose to adopt neutrality.[66]

3.   Assuming Neutrality

Some small states see neutrality as the best way of defending their independence and sovereignty. Michael Waltzer defines neutrality as "a collective and voluntary form of noncombatancy."[67] Efraim

---

[64] Reiter and Gaertner, *Small States and Alliance,* 3.

[65] Reiter and Gaertner, *Small States and Alliance,* 3.

[66] Reiter and Gaertner, *Small States and Alliance,* 3.

[67] Michael Waltzer, *Just and Unjust Wars. A Moral Argument with Historical Illustration, Third Edition,* (New

Karsh states that neutrality is "the status of a state during a specific war in which it has decided not to intervene."[68] Robert L. Rothstein explains the reasons a small state might choose to assume neutrality: "One reason is that small powers tend to rely on the hope that they can be protected by their own insignificance. If they can appear detached enough, and disinterested enough, and if they can convincingly indicate that they are too powerless to affect the issue, they hope the storm will pass them by."[69] Like Rothstein, Martin Wright writes of small states that "their hope is to lie low and escape notice."[70] To be effective, however, a small state's assumed neutrality requires the combatants' agreement and approval. These arrangements are usually based on the common interests of the belligerents. When these interests cease to exist, it usually brings an end to the viability of small-state

---

York: Basic Books, 2000), 234.

[68] Efraim Karsh, *Neutrality and Small States*, (Worcester: Billing and Sons Ltd, 1988), 26.

[69] Rothstein, *Alliances and Small Powers*, 26.

[70] Wight, Power Politics, 160.

neutrality. History provides many cases when neutrality was either honored or disregarded by major powers. For example, during the Peloponnesian War, Melos, a small merchant island, assumed neutrality. Athens viewed Melos as strategically important, and when it refused to join the Athenian alliance, it was attacked.[71] During the Second World War, Nazi Germany, based on its temporary interests, honored the neutrality of Switzerland and Sweden and disregarded that of Belgium, Luxembourg, and the Netherlands.[72]

As these examples show, neutrality as a homeland-defense strategy can work only in two situations. First, if the small state manages to sustain its unimportance and impartiality during a conflict. Second, as in the case of Switzerland and Sweden, if it combines geographical advantages with a significant, but not necessarily great, military

---

[71] Thucydides, *History of the Peloponnesian War*, translated by Rex Warner (New York: Penguin Group, 1972), 212-222.

[72] William L. Shirer, *The Rise and Fall of the Third Reich: A History of Nazi Germany*, (New York: Simon and Schuster, 1990), 721-723.

power—which raises the cost of attack to an unacceptable level. Although this second scenario seems ideal, the same problems surface as in the case of imitation. That is the reason neutrality has remained primarily a European phenomenon, in countries, including Sweden and Switzerland, with significant terrain advantages and the financial ability to exploit this alternative.[73] On the other hand, if a small state does not possess these resources, it still can choose the fourth type of homeland-defense strategy, which is to acquire weapons of mass destruction.

4. Acquiring Weapons of Mass Destruction

The last traditional homeland-defense strategy for small states is based on the possession of weapons of mass destructions, or WMDs, as a deterrent. Although this strategy could stand alone, it is usually combined with one of the above-mentioned strategies. When states believe that they

---

[73] Karsh, *Neutrality and Small States*, 26.

cannot compete with the conventional, or in some cases, nuclear capabilities of their enemy, they can try to acquire some type of WMD.[74] The most important advantage of these weapon systems is that they significantly increase any state's deterrent power and, in case of conflict, provide "the ability to inflict damage that is wholly disproportionate to their conventional military capabilities."[75] These seem significant and achievable capabilities for small states that cannot sustain large armies, cannot join an alliance, and do not want to assume neutrality. However the biggest challenge of WMDs is the acquisition of materiel and the establishment of necessary infrastructure.[76]

Since the fall of the Soviet Union, the proliferation of WMDs has become a prominent

---

[74] Pakistan and India both possess nuclear weapons to equalize their destructive power.

[75] U.S. Congress, Office of "Technology Assessment, *Proliferation of Weapons of Mass Destruction: Assessing the Rish, OTA-ISC-559,* (Washington, DC: U.S. Government Printing Office, August 1993), 2.

[76] U.S. Congress, Office of "Technology Assessment, *Proliferation of Weapons of Mass Destruction,* 9.

national-security concern of the major powers. Iran and North Korea's nuclear programs, the Pakistani–Indian nuclear arms race, Israel's secret program, and the politically instable and economically wracked former Soviet Union members have brought increased attention to the issue.[77] International cooperation on the issue of proliferation is at a high never seen before. The Nuclear Non-Proliferation Treaty, which dates back to 5 March 1970, has been signed by 189 states that have renounced nuclear weapons.[78] A hundred and twenty-five countries have even stepped forward and given up chemical weapons completely by joining the Biological Weapons Convention,[79] and 140 states have signed the Chemical Weapons Convention.[80] These agreements established a

---

[77] U.S. Congress, Office of "Technology Assessment, *Proliferation of Weapons of Mass Destruction,* 1.

[78] United States Information Pertaining to the Treaty on the Non-Proliferation of Nuclear Weapons, 2010, 2-7. accessed October 06, 2011. http://www.state.gov/documents/organization/141928.pdf

[79] U.S. Congress, Office of "Technology Assessment, *Proliferation of Weapons of Mass Destruction,* 2.

[80] U.S. Congress, Office of "Technology Assessment,

strong international norm for cooperation against WMDs, which makes it very difficult for a small state to acquire all the necessary elements of an effective WMD capability. The difficulty of buying materiel, hiring the proper subject-matter experts, building the necessary infrastructure, and buying or developing the proper delivery means[81] are financial challenges for a small state, and, because of the international environment, even the effort to acquire WMDs can bring disproportionate disadvantages that trump the possible advantages of possessing such a capability. These international agreements contain numerous provisions that make even the intent of acquisition painful for any state or, conversely, beneficial for those who abandon WMDs. Preventive measures can include economic

---

Proliferation of Weapons of Mass Destruction, 2.

[81] The overall cost of overtly producing one nuclear bomb a year is about $200 million, biological weapons, enough for a large arsenal may cost less than $10 million, while chemical arsenal for substantial military capability (hundreds of tons of agent) likely to cost tens ofmillions of dollars.

U.S. Congress, Office of "Technology Assessment, *Proliferation of Weapons of Mass Destruction,* 11.

sanctions, diplomatic isolation, or even preventive military attack,[82] while the rewards for giving up WMD programs can range from economic to military-development assistance and significant financial support.[83]

While the possession of WMDs gives great power to small states, as in the case of North Korea, the road is highly risky and full of obstacles. Because of the contemporary international environment, small states have to risk all the value they wanted to protect in the first place by acquiring WMDs. For those states who believe they have no other choice than to compete with their adversaries and would lose against them anyway, this path may be the one; but for those who do not want to risk economic sanctions and "preventive" military intervention, there may be yet another way to protect their homeland.

---

[82] U.S. Congress, Office of "Technology Assessment, *Proliferation of Weapons of Mass Destruction,* 5-6.

[83] U.S. Congress, Office of "Technology Assessment, *Proliferation of Weapons of Mass Destruction,* 5-6.

C. PROFESSIONAL IRREGULAR FORCE THEORY

In his book, *Theory of International Politics*, Kenneth Waltz argues that in the current competitive international environment, states "socialize" to similar strategies. He states that "The fate of each state depends on its responses to what other states do. The possibility that conflict will be conducted by force leads to competition in the arts and the instruments of force. Competition produces a tendency toward the sameness of the competitors."[84] His thoughts on the idea of "competition in the arts and the instruments of force" and the reconsideration of the importance of "sameness" can give a starting point for small states to rethink their understanding about defensive strategy.

Since the end of the Cold War, the gap between states' military capabilities has been opening with increased speed, to the disadvantage

---

[84] Kenneth N. Waltz, *Theory of International Politics,* (New York: McGraw-Hill, 1979), 127.

of the smaller states, whose financial and technical capabilities do not allow them to compete effectively. Since this process has created a huge asymmetry between the military capabilities of small and large states, the weaker side's answer to this challenge should not be "sameness," but perhaps "asymmetry."

This thesis suggests that if a small state faces an enemy with superior military capabilities, the only way for the small state to win during a conflict is to take away its opponent's advantages, or make them irrelevant. For those small states that understand how inadequate the imitation of large-state militaries is in the contemporary environment and how much risk the acquisition of WMDs contains, or who want to find a solution more self reliant than the notion of collective security, an analysis of Ivan Arreguín-Toft's theory on asymmetric conflicts may usefully answer how a small state should defend itself.

Ivan Arreguín-Toft, in *How the Weak Win Wars: A Theory of Asymmetric Conflict,* presents some valuable starting points for small states to consider. Arreguín-Toft states that the final outcome of any conflict is the result of the interaction of the adversaries' strategies. He argues that the confronting strategies can be reduced to two distinctive forms: direct and indirect approaches.[85] Direct strategies focus on the destruction of the enemy's armed forces and through this, its capacity to continue fighting. The indirect strategy aims for the destruction of the enemy's will to fight.[86] This concept was introduced by B. H. Liddell Hart in his book, *Strategy, the Indirect Approach*. Liddell Hart states that "in war, as in wrestling, the attempt to throw the opponent without loosening his foothold and balance can only result in self-exhaustion."[87] He further explains that "victory by such a method can only be possible through an immense margin of

---

[85] Ivan Arreguín-Toft, *How the weak win wars: The Theory of Asymmetric Conflict*, (New York: Cambridge University Press, 2005), 105.

[86] Arreguín-Toft, *How the weak win wars: The Theory of Asymmetric Conflict*, 105.

[87] Basil H. Liddell Hart, *Strategy, The Indirect Approach*, (Natraj Publisher, 2003), 5.

superior strength in some form, and, even so, tends to lose decisiveness."[88] Through his studies of history, Liddell Hart finds that "in almost all the decisive campaigns the dislocation of the enemy's psychological and physical balance has been the vital prelude to a successful attempt at his overthrow. This dislocation has been produced by a strategic indirect approach."[89] Arreguín-Toft found that when in an asymmetric conflict both sides use the same strategic approach, either direct against direct or indirect against indirect, the stronger actor almost always wins, since "there is nothing to mediate or deflect a strong actor's power advantage."[90] Decades earlier, Mao Zedong came to the same conclusion when he stated that "defeat is the invariable outcome where native forces fight with inferior weapons against modernized forces on the latter's terms."[91] By contrast, Arreguín-Toft

---

[88] Liddell Hart, *Strategy, The Indirect Approach,* 5.

[89] Liddell Hart, *Strategy, The Indirect Approach,* 5.

[90] Arreguín-Toft, *How the weak win wars: The Theory of Asymmetric Conflict,* 105.

[91] Andrew Mack, "Why Big Nations Lose Small Wars,"

states that when opposite strategic approaches interact, it implies the victory of the weaker actor, since the stronger party's advantages are deflected.

To further understand the strength and possible implications of the above points, one needs to see the patterns of military development that are influencing the contemporary world. After the Second World War, two strategic mindsets emerged. The first was the "blitzkrieg pattern," which was based on the deployment of large conventional, mechanized forces to destroy the enemy's military and capture its territory without huge "battles of annihilation."[92] This pattern was introduced by the world's leading militaries, including the United States, the Soviet Union, and most of the European states. The way post-Second World War conflicts have been handled by these militaries, including the Korean, Vietnam, Afghan, and Iraq wars, suggest that this pattern still has

---

Word Politics, Volume: 27, Issue: 2, (1975): 176.

[92] Arreguín-Toft, *How the weak win wars: The Theory of Asymmetric Conflict*, 106.

overwhelming influence on the military doctrine of those states. Another proof of the effects of this pattern is the research and development competition among those states, which still pursue better airplanes, tanks, boats, missiles, etc. The other pattern was guerrilla warfare, which emphasized protracted war against a superior enemy. The model was imitated in countries like China, Algeria, Vietnam, Cuba, and recently, successfully in Iraq and Afghanistan. Arreguín-Toft found that when the blitzkrieg and guerrilla warfare "interact systematically; strong actors should lose more often."[93] To support this statement, he presented two important historical data sets regarding the outcome of asymmetric wars between 1800 and 1998. The first result was that the weaker side won 30 percent of the time. The second result showed that the frequency of the weaker-side victory

[93] Arreguin-Toft, *How the weak win wars: The Theory of Asymmetric Conflict*, 106.

[94] Arreguin-Toft, *How the weak win wars: The Theory of Asymmetric Conflict*, 96.

increased over time. After the Second World War, between 1950 and 1998, 55 percent of asymmetric conflicts were won by the weak side. [94] If one understands the theory of Arreguín-Toft and accepts what the historical data suggest, then it may be worthwhile for small states to consider turning their attention away from the idea of "sameness." They should look for a less usual, less generally accepted, but possibly more effective solution, which should include the integration of guerrilla warfare and other irregular-warfare methods into their homeland-defense strategy.

As a starting point, small states should remember the exchange recounted earlier between Colonel Harry Summers and Colonel Tu, on how North Vietnamese forces had never defeated the American troops on the battlefield, but that this fact was irrelevant to the end results of the war. This and many other historical examples encourage the discovery of the possible conditions under which a "professional irregular force" approach should be considered by a small state. To do so, it is necessary to understand the suggested approach in detail.

The "professional" part of the suggested approach means that the actual defense force, like most countries' conventional forces, has to be organized, trained, equipped, and sustained as an active-duty military organization in peacetime. Its members have to be fulltime soldiers and need to be continuously trained for irregular warfare. Background organizations such as schools and training centers need to be established, supportive infrastructure needs to be built, and necessary resources have to be allocated towards one single goal: to serve the irregular homeland-defense strategy. The closest successful example is the strategy followed by Hezbollah in south Lebanon between 2000 and 2006 as a preparation for the Second Lebanese War in 2006.[95]

Continuing with definitions, one needs to

---

[95] Scott C. Farquhar, *Back to Basics, A Study of the Second Lebanon War and Operation Cast Lead,* (Fort Leavenworth, Kansas: Combat Studies Institute Press, 2009), 6-10.

understand the meaning of irregular warfare. According to the United States' Army's irregular-warfare (IW) joint operating concept, irregular warfare is "a violent struggle among state and non-state actors for legitimacy and influence over the relevant populations. IW favors indirect and asymmetric approaches, though it may employ the full range of military and other capabilities, in order to erode an adversary's power, influence, and will."[96] It also suggests that irregular warfare "includes a wide variety of indirect operations and activities that occur in isolation or within "traditional" inter-state combat operations."[97] Although these definitions are very recent, the use of "nontraditional" ways to defeat an enemy "is as old as the history of warfare."[98] The use of irregular tactics was probably first recorded in the fifteenth century B.C., when the Hittite king Mursilis wrote

---

[96] Irregular warfare (IW) Joint Operating Concept (JOC), Version 1, Department of Defense, 2007, 6.

[97] Joint operating concept (JOC), 9.

[98] Lewis H. Gann, *Guerrillas in History*, (Stanford, CA: Hoover Institution Press, 1971), 78.

in a letter that "the irregulars did not dare to attack me in the daylight and preferred to fall on me by night."[99] Since this ancient moment, numerous written reports suggest the extensive use of irregular methods during wars, across time and place. History also suggests that irregular warfare does not belong to any "particular ideology, century, or culture."[100] Irregular fighters have had many names, such as guerrillas, insurgents, partisans, paramilitary, freedom fighters, and the like, and despite their many differences, they have fought similarly. The common ground for those who capitalize on irregular methods is confrontation with numerically larger, usually more modern and professional, conventional armies. Despite its numerous appearances, irregular warfare was not of much interest in modern military studies for a long time. Lewis H. Gann may provide a hint about the reasons when he states about partisan warfare that

---

[99] Laqueur, *Guerrilla Warfare,* 3.

[100] Anthony J. Joes, *Guerrilla Warfare. A Historical, Biographical, and Bibliographical Sourcebook,* (Westport: Greenwood Press, 1996), 4.

"it is based essentially on the precepts of common sense, and requires no particular mystique for its elucidation."[101] Although the extended use of irregular warfare tactics in wars in North America, Russia, and Spain[102] caught the attention of some military theorists, including Antoine-Henri Jomini, they nevertheless concluded that it was only a secondary technique and not a decisive form of warfare.

This view started to change with Carl von Clausewitz's "people's war" theory and was further developed at the beginning of the 20th century when the use of irregular warfare became more and more successful in conflicts, especially in the colonial era. Conflicts like the Boer, the Algerian, and Vietnam wars are examples of the integrated use of irregular methods. Since then, the use of

---

[101] Gann, *Guerrillas in History*, 78.

[102] The term guerrilla is originated from the small groups of Spanish rebels who effectively fought against Napoleon's forces during the occupation of Spain from 1808 to 1814.

John Arquilla, *Insurgents, Raiders and Bandits: How Masters of Irregular Warfare Have Shaped Our World,* (Maryland: The Rowman and Littlefield Publishing Group Inc, 2011), 4.

irregular warfare has become more common, and numerous conflicts, such as the First Russo–Chechen War, the Afghan *mujahideen* resistance against the Soviet Union, and the Second Lebanese War, provide examples of the success of irregular warfare and irregular forces. These historical events are crucial for small states, since they can reveal the dynamics of irregular warfare and provide directions about how to develop them even further.

What follows is a series of six historical case studies focusing on military conflicts in which irregular warfare methods played a major part in the defensive strategy against an aggressor state using a conventional, orthodox military approach. The analysis of these six conflicts will identify the key reasons for the success or failure of the irregular forces and will highlight the conditions under which it is preferable for a small state to consider the introduction of the proposed "professional irregular force" strategy.

CHAPTER 3
THE AMERICAN REVOLUTIONARY WAR

A. BACKGROUND

Britain's 1763 victory over France in the Seven Years' War ended the competition for the rule of North America, but set the stage for a new conflict with the British colonies. Tension had been rising between the British government and the American colonists for more than ten years before the actual start of the American Revolution in 1775. To finance the British troops stationed in North America, the imperial authorities took steps to raise taxes in the colonies. These attempts, including the Stamp Act[103] in 1765 and the Tea Act[104] in 1773, caused many protests among the colonists, who responded by demanding representation in the British parliament and extended rights, like those of other British subjects. In response to violent events

---

[103] Anthony James Joes, *America and Guerrilla Warfare,* (Lexington: The University Press of Kentucky, 2000), 7.

[104] Benjamin W. Labaree, *The Boston Tea Party*, (Boston: Northeastern University Press, 1979), 67.

in Massachusetts, including the Boston Massacre in 1770[105] and the Boston Tea Party in December 1773[106], Parliament introduced a series of measures to reassert the empire's authority. In response to these events, in September 1774, some colonial delegates gathered in Philadelphia to discuss their grievances against the British. This meeting, known as the First Continental Congress, did not demand independence yet, but refused to accept any taxation without proper parliamentary representation and created a declaration of rights due every citizen, including those of liberty, assembly, property, and trial by jury. The members of this congress decided to meet again in May 1775 to discuss any additional necessary actions, but by that time, events have sped up dramatically. On April 19, 1775, in incidents known as the battles of Lexington and Concord, local militia confronted

---

[105] Hiller B. Zobel, *The Boston Massacre*, (New York: W.W. Norton & Company, 1970), 196.

[106] John K Alexander, *Samuel Adams: America's Revolutionary Politician*, (Lanham: Rowman & Littlefield, 2002), 125-126.

and routed a British troop column.[107] That day's bloody confrontation led to the outbreak of the American Revolutionary War.

During the Second Continental Congress, which gathered May 10, 1775, the delegates supported the establishment of a continental army and appointed George Washington as commander. The new military force soon met its first challenge when the war's first major battle took place at Breed's Hill in Boston. The battle ended in British victory; however, the heavy casualties inflicted by the colonials on the British forces encouraged the revolutionary cause and resulted in the British being locked down in Boston for the rest of the year.[108] Afterwards, the British withdrew; so in both a tactical and a strategic sense, the American forces did well.

Any chance of a compromise between the British Crown and the colonists ended when on July 4, 1776, the Continental Congress began creating a

---

[107] Mark V. Kwasny, *Washington's Partisan War, 1775–1783,* (Ohio: Kent, 1996), 5.

[108] Kwasny, *Washington's Partisan War,* 10.

new nation by issuing the Declaration of Independence.[109] In response, the outraged British government sent a large fleet and more than 34,000 troops to New York to put down the rebellion.

The following months brought successes and failures for both sides. In September, British redcoats forced Washington to evacuate his units from New York City to avoid the loss of his whole army. On Christmas night, by pushing across the Delaware River, Washington fought successfully back in Trenton, New Jersey, and also won a victory at Princeton before the army made its winter camp at Morristown. The year 1777 brought the British master plan to "divide the colonies two parts and then subdue one part at a time, effectively doubling the power of the available British forces."[110] The goal of this strategy was the isolation of New England from Pennsylvania and the south, since it was seen by the British as the southern center of the rebellion. General John Burgoyne's army

---

[109] Joes, *America and Guerrilla Warfare,* 9.
[110] Joes, *America and Guerrilla Warfare,* 13.

maneuvered from Canada to meet with General William Howe's army of New York to combine forces. While General Burgoyne defeated the Americans in July by taking Fort Ticonderoga, Howe abandoned the original plan and turned his troops away from New York to attack Washington near the Chesapeake Bay. Howe's decision left General Burgoyne's troops exposed and led to his devastating defeat on September 19, by American troops under General Horatio Gates near Saratoga, New York. On October 7, General Burgoyne's army suffered another defeat at Bemis Heights, known as the Second Battle of Saratoga. Burgoyne surrendered his army on October 17.[111]

The victory at Saratoga was a turning point of the war. Following this battle, France, which had secretly provided support to the rebels since 1776, joined the war openly on the American side, though not officially declaring war on Great Britain till June 1778. With this alliance, the previously

---

[111] Richard M Ketchum, *Saratoga: Turning Point of America's Revolutionary War*, (Henry Holt, 1997), 67.

internal conflict for the British Empire became a world war.[112]

Having replaced General Howe as supreme commander, Sir Henry Clinton wanted to withdraw his troops from Philadelphia to New York, on June 28, 1778. Washington's army confronted them at Monmouth, New Jersey. The fight ended in a draw, but Clinton got his army to New York. On July 8, a French fleet arrived off the Atlantic coast, ready to fight the British. In late July, a colonial and French attack on Newport, Rhode Island, failed, and the war more or less settled into a stalemate phase in the north.[113]

In 1778, London decided to shift its main effort to the south with an attempt to conquer the southern colonies. "There was a widespread view in London that the southern colonies were full of loyal subjects just waiting for assistance to free

---

[112] Don Higginbotham, *The War of American Independence: Military Attitudes, Policies, and Practice, 1763–1789,* (Northeastern University Press, 1983), 188-198.

[113] Higginbotham, *The War of American Independence,* 175-188.

themselves from the oppression of the disloyal minority."[114] The British first occupied Georgia in 1779, then captured Charleston, South Carolina, in May 1780. The main British army, led by Lord Charles Cornwallis, crushed General Horatio Gates's command at Camden in August. Soon after Camden, General Nathaniel Greene replaced Gates as supreme commander of the colonies' southern forces. General Greene's understanding of the situation, his knowledge of the strength and weaknesses of his own troops and the enemy's, and his masterly combination of regulars and irregular forces, turned the fight around.[115] By the fall of 1781, Greene's strategy forced Cornwallis to withdraw to Virginia's Yorktown peninsula. Washington, supported by a French army, marched to Yorktown with around 14,000 soldiers. At the same time, a fleet of 36 French warships sailed to the shores of Yorktown to prevent British

---

[114] Joes, *America and Guerrilla Warfare,* 13.

[115] John Arquilla, *From Troy to Entebbe. Special Operations in Ancient and Modern Times,* (University Press of America, 1996), 84.

reinforcement or evacuation. The trap, and the overwhelming Franco–American force advantage, forced Cornwallis to surrender on October 19.[116]

Although British forces remained in Charleston and the main British army held New York City, the victory at Yorktown meant triumph for the American colonies. Neither side took decisive action for the next two years. The British withdrawal from Charleston and Savannah in 1782 marked the end of the armed conflict. Representatives from the American colonies and the British Empire signed a peace treaty in Paris on September 3, 1783, which officially recognized the United States as an independent country.[117]

B. IRREGULAR STRATEGY

The American colonies started the war without a standing military force, allies, or significant outside support and faced an enemy that had the best army and navy of its time.[118] To

---

[116] Arquilla, *From Troy to Entebbe,* 85-89.

[117] Joes, *America and Guerrilla Warfare,* 46.

defeat this enemy, the colonies needed to take away the adversary's advantages. Knowing their own weaknesses and the strength of the British forces, the rebels did not have the option of fighting conventionally.

Earlier history, such as in the Seven Years' War, showed that the Americans had considerable irregular knowledge and experience. The citizen soldiers "were also among the pioneers of accurate, aimed shooting, a practice that was not yet widely accepted in the military manuals of the period."[119] They also had the ability to conduct military operations by living in the field and hiding in swamps and wilderness.[120] Although these capabilities could be observed as early as the first clash in Lexington and surfaced during many engagements throughout the war, the proper strategic use of these citizen soldiers and their irregular tactics was a challenging issue for most of

---

[118] Arquilla, *Insurgents, Raiders and Bandits,* 30.

[119] Laqueur, *Guerrilla Warfare,* 21.

[120] Arquilla, *Insurgents, Raiders and Bandits,* 30.

the colonial leaders through the entire conflict. At the beginning of the war, the newly appointed commander-in-chief, George Washington, was advised by Major General Charles Lee[121] that "a war fought to attain revolutionary purposes ought to be waged revolutionary manner, calling on an armed populace to rise in what a later generation would call guerrilla war."[122] But Washington completely rejected the idea of irregular war and was in favor of conventionalizing the Continental military to create a European-type force.[123] Washington addressed his opinion about the militia at the beginning of the conflict, "All General Officers agree that no Dependence can be put on the Militia for a Continuance in Camp, or Regularity and Discipline during the short Time they may stay."[124] Although his conventional mindset did not change too much during the war, the militia and

---

[121] Arquilla, *Insurgents, Raiders and Bandits,* 30.

[122] Arquilla, *Insurgents, Raiders and Bandits,* 30.

[123] Arquilla, *Insurgents, Raiders and Bandits,* 30.

[124] Kwasny, *Washington's Partisan War,* xi.

their irregular warfare successes, especially in the southern colonies, forced Washington to change his opinion. "The Militia of this Country must be considered as the Palladium of our security, and the first effectual resort in case of hostility..."[125] Washington's second in command, General Nathaniel Greene, had a different view about the strategic applicability of the militia and their irregular tactics. When he succeeded General Horatio Gates, on December 2, 1780, as the commander of the southern army,[126] General Greene implemented a strategy that integrated irregular and conventional operations and created a symbiotic relationship in the southern theater.

For Greene, the task of defeating General Cornwallis and reconquering the three southern colonies seemed impossible. When he arrived, the southern army consisted of 2,300 men, with only 800 fit to fight. The army also had only three days' supplies of rations. The camps were dirty, the army

---

[125] Kwasny, *Washington's Partisan War,* xi

[126] Arquilla, *From Troy to Entebbe,* 84.

was short on supplies, and morale was low.[127] Facing Greene was the strategically most competent British commander in North America, General Cornwallis, with his numerically superior, conventionally trained, professional army. General Greene realized that he needed something unexpected and different from the normal "bookish" military strategy to turn the odds around. He decided to create a combined irregular and conventional strategy. The goal was not to go for a swift, decisive victory over General Cornwallis, but to fight to buy time and keep the revolutionary cause alive. General Greene understood Washington's theory that "the war must be defensive in character that the colonists— even with the help of the French — were not capable of facing the British in open warfare."[128] General Greene's famous quote, "We fight, get beat, rise and fight again,"[129] describes the essence of this theory.

---

[127] Arquilla, *From Troy to Entebbe*, 84.

[128] Laqueur, *Guerrilla Warfare*, 21.

[129] Arquilla, *From Troy to Entebbe*, 89.

General Greene understood that the southern army in its current condition could not fight conventional battles as one single force. He decided to go against common military logic and divided his already weak force into two parts. At the same time, he contacted guerrilla leaders such as Francis Marion, known as the Swamp Fox, and Thomas Sumter, the Gamecock,[130] to coordinate their operations with his conventional main forces. The idea of Greene's strategy was to integrate irregular actions and conventional operations to impose as many casualties and as much loss of materiel as possible, to make the price of the British operations so high as to become impossible to sustain. The following abstract from a letter from General Greene to Francis Marion is a clear depiction of his intentions. "Gen. Sumter is desired to call out all the militia of South Carolina and employ them in destroying the enemy's stores and perplexing their affairs in the state. Please to communicate and concert with him your future

---

[130] Laqueur, *Guerrilla Warfare,* 20.

operations until we have a better opportunity to have more free intercourse. Great activity is necessary to keep the spirits of the people from sinking, as well as to alarm the enemy respecting the safety of their posts."[131]

The irregulars also collected valuable information behind enemy lines and suppressed Tories from supporting the British. Through harassment of the British forces with quick raids against outposts and lines of communications, the irregulars created the feeling in the British forces that they could be attacked anytime and anywhere. At the same time, the colonial conventional forces maneuvered across the region to pose enough of a threat to Cornwallis to prevent him from turning all his power against the rebel irregulars.

General Greene hoped that Cornwallis was going to divide his own army and by that means make his forces more vulnerable to raids and

[131] William Dobein James, *Swamp Fox: General Francis Marion and his Irregular Fighters of the American Revolutionary War*, (St Petersburg: Red and Black Publishers, 2010), 136.

harassment. To increase the effectiveness of guerrilla operations, Lieutenant Colonel Henry "Light Horse Harry" Lee and his cavalry from the main southern army joined Francis Marion. To support the irregulars' actions, the conventional forces kept maneuvering on the battlefield and engaging the British only when favorable. Even in opportunities for potential victory, such as Hobkirk's Hill or Eutaw Springs in 1781, Greene never took the risk of fully committing his forces.[132]

Greene's strategy paid off in a very short time. The British had great difficulties in countering this strategy. Cornwallis and his army paid so great a price for trying to destroy the southern colonial army and the irregular forces that it became impossible to sustain any further effective military operations in the southern states. Despite never winning a clear tactical victory, General Greene won the campaign in the south strategically by an effective combination of conventional and irregular strategy.

---

[132] Arquilla, *From Troy to Entebbe,* 85-87.

C. ORGANIZATION AND LEADERSHIP

The organization of the irregular forces never followed a definite pattern. Marion and Sumter's forces remained fluid and flexible during the entire war. Throughout the campaign, the men of the irregular forces were supposedly enlisted for the duration of the war, but in many cases, after they subdued the enemy or chased away the local British loyalists, these rebels returned to their homes. Francis Marion usually led a small, mobile force of 20 to 70 men.[133] He rarely led exactly the same men for more than two weeks.[134] Thomas Sumter, on the other hand, usually commanded a couple hundred men at a time; but even his forces were very flexible. In August 1780, his camp was almost completely destroyed by the British, yet within a week he reorganized and was back in action.[135] Temporary task forces, organized from

[133] "Francis Marion" Encyclopedia of World Biography. 2004. *Encyclopedia.com.*, accessed August 25, 2011, http://www.encyclopedia.com/doc/1G2-3404704217.html.

[134] Joes, *America and Guerrilla Warfare.* 39.

conventional and irregular units, were also frequently used, such as in Lee, Marion, and Sumter's joint attack on a British supply depot at Monck's Corner, just outside Charleston, in 1781. Other examples included Lee's and Marion's raids along the Congaree River.

To achieve success with irregular forces, the leaders needed special personalities and adaptation skills that were uncommon at the time. General Greene started his campaign with an extraordinary ability to understand the situation and to see strength where others could see only weakness. As one of his officers explained after Greene took command: "by the following morning [Greene] understood better than Gates [had] done in the whole period of his command."[136] He had the ability to adapt to a challenging situation and exploit the possibilities. He threw away conventional military thinking and implemented an unexpected, and, for the times, illogical, but

---

[135] Joes, *America and Guerrilla Warfare.* 40.

[136] Arquilla, *From Troy to Entebbe,* 84.

effective strategy. To succeed, General Greene also needed capable guerrilla commanders. "The leaders of the southern irregulars were almost all veterans of the Cherokee campaign of 1761."[137] In that war they learned several key principles, which proved vital during the Revolutionary War, including the importance of cover, silent movement, and accurate, aimed shooting. The two most significant guerrilla leaders were Francis Marion and Thomas Sumter, controversial personalities who fought very effectively to support the revolutionary cause.

Francis Marion served in the provincial forces as an officer and fought the first years of the war as a conventional leader. After the British retook Charleston in May, 1780, ending the formal American resistance in South Carolina, Marion refused to surrender, took to the swamps, and started a guerrilla war against the British. He " kept the flame of resistance to tyranny alight in the south during the darkest days of the Revolution."[138] One

---

[137] Laqueur, *Guerrilla Warfare*, 20.
[138] Joes, *America and Guerrilla Warfare*, 36.

of the key components of his success was his ability to understand British tactics. With this knowledge, he exploited their weaknesses while avoiding their strengths. He and his men moved like phantoms. Mobility was the basic foundation of their tactics. Marion was quick in planning and execution, and was impossible to catch. Marion shared hardship with his men; "since his men had no tents, he slept also in the open."[139] General Greene admired his achievements by writing the following about Marion:

> History affords no instance wherein an officer has kept possession of a country under so many disadvantages as you have. Surrounded on every side with superior force, hunted from every quarter by veteran troops, you have found means to elude all their attempts, and to keep alive the expiring hopes of an oppressed militia, when all succor seemed to be cut off. To fight the enemy bravely with a prospect of victory is nothing; but to fight with intrepidity under the constant impression of defeat, and inspire irregular troops to do it, is a talent peculiar to yourself.[140]

---

[139] Joes, *America and Guerrilla Warfare*, 37.

With his previous conventional officer's background, Marion had no problem with authority and following the orders of General Greene. This ability resulted in the effective coordination and integration of his forces with General Greene's conventional units.

The other significant irregular leader in the southern campaign was Thomas Sumter. Although he held a rank of a colonel in the Continental Army from 1775 to 1776, he was frustrated in his military activities and returned to his plantation. After the fall of Charleston in 1780, the British burned his house to the ground. Sumter was then elected general by the South Carolina militia in June 1780 and immediately launched a guerrilla campaign against the British forces. He was famous for keeping his men busy. When they were not fighting, General Sumter continuously trained them "through swimming and running, leaping and wrestling."[141]

[140] Joes, *America and Guerrilla Warfare,* 38.
[141] Joes, *America and Guerrilla Warfare,* 41.

His unit won the "hearts and minds" of the locals by distributing food to the civilian population. General Sumter and his irregulars provided vital intelligence to General Greene, handed over large amounts of confiscated supplies, and sometimes served as a screening force to cover the maneuvers of the main forces.[142] However General Sumter, unlike Francis Marion, had problems accepting the authority of the conventional commanders. Although his occasional subordination created some frictions between Greene's forces and his own irregulars, as the following letter abstract from General Greene to Francis Marion indicates, they could count on General Sumter whenever he was needed. "The army will march tomorrow, and I hope you will be prepared to support its operations with a considerable force; Gen. Sumter is written to, and I doubt not will be prepared to cooperate with us."[143]

---

[142] Joes, *America and Guerrilla Warfare,* 41.

[143] Dobein, *Swamp Fox,* 142.

SANDOR FABIAN

D. INTERNAL FACTORS

Irregular forces conducted their operations in three distinguishable ways during the American Revolutionary War. First, they operated independently from conventional units, but still in support of larger strategic purposes, like almost all the irregular units in the south had before General Greene contacted them and suggested an integration of efforts. Second, they operated in coordination with conventional commanders to support conventional forces, as in Marion, Sumter, and Lee's attack on the British supply depot at Monck's Corner, outside Charleston.[144] Finally, irregular forces operated under the direct control of a conventional commander as part of a conventional force, like Francis Marion's joining General Greene at Eutaw Springs.[145] When irregulars joined the conventional forces, they were often placed in the front line[146] and fought as conventional soldiers,

---

[144] Arquilla, *From Troy to Entebbe,* 90.
[145] Arquilla, *From Troy to Entebbe,* 90.
[146] Arquilla, *From Troy to Entebbe,* 90.

but it was when they operated independently that they proved their real effectiveness.

The first of the significant internal factors was the type of tactics used. The American rebels, unlike their British conventional counterparts, were trained hunters. They had the ability to sustain themselves in the field and had extensive knowledge of the local terrain in which they operated. Since the British used conventional military tactics at every level of engagement, the unconventional mindset of the guerrillas created, in many cases, great advantages for the colonial units. Their tactics included the application of small, horse-mounted, hit-and-run parties and the conduct of night attacks and operations during extreme weather. Some of the British soldiers, including Banastre Tarleton, were skilled in these types of tactics, but for the average, conventionally trained British soldier and leaders, they were unfamiliar. Lt. Col. John W. T. Watson explained his failure to catch Francis Marion in March 1781 by claiming, "he would not fight like a gentleman or a Christian."[147]

One of the most important irregular tactics was directly linked to the British strategy of controlling the interior areas by establishing outposts. General Cornwallis constructed a line of small forts that primarily depended on supplies from Charleston. This provided a great opportunity for attacks on smaller British forces and their lines of communications. These harassing operations created fear among the British and led to an increase of forces devoted to searching those areas and securing the outposts. The attacks on the lines of communications resulted in large quantities of seized enemy materiel and denied the British the ability to properly resupply their troops. Two examples of this method were the inability to transport materials on the Santee River from the coast to the interior by the end of October 1780[148] and the rescue of 150 American prisoners during an attack on a British patrol.[149]

---

[147] "Francis Marion" Encyclopedia of World Biography.

[148] Joes, *America and Guerrilla Warfare,* 39.

[149] "Francis Marion" Encyclopedia of World Biography.

The effectiveness of irregular tactics was further increased by conducting operations at night and in severe weather. One of Francis Marion's favorite tactics was to approach the encamped enemy at night and attack them from the middle while closing down any escape route on the sides, then retreating swiftly.[150] Fighting at night and attacking an encamped enemy were both unexpected and very unconventional at the time. Regarding this type of operation, General Henry Lee wrote about Francis Marion, "he struck unperceived; and retiring to those hidden retreats selected by himself...he placed his corps not only out of the reach of his foe, but often out of the discovery of his friends."[151]

To effectively support American strategic goals and deny the British local support, the irregulars conducted many operations to suppress the loyalists and the Crown's most reliable Indian allies, the Tories. Both Marion and Sumter

---

[150] Joes, *America and Guerrilla Warfare,* 37.

[151] Joes, *America and Guerrilla Warfare,* 37.

conducted raids on British loyalists to frighten them out of enlisting, always threatening further punishment. Sumter used Catawba Indians to track loyalists who hid in the swamps or forests. Small search parties hunted down and killed many loyalists.[152]

The second important internal factor was the role of intelligence. The irregular forces' ability to move around the battlefield quickly and their knowledge of the terrain and weather of the country proved vital assets for collecting information on the composition and disposition of British forces and maneuvers. The constant attacks on outposts and lines of communications provided a large number of prisoners and seized material. The exploitation of these often allowed the irregulars to achieve an information advantage over the British. This ability was further increased by the brutal behavior of the British forces, which "antagonized the local population."[153] Many of those who were neutral

---

[152] Joes, *America and Guerrilla Warfare,* 41.
[153] Laqueur, *Guerrilla Warfare,* 21.

earlier in the war turned to the cause of the revolution.

E. EXTERNAL FACTORS

The terrain and weather of North America were the most significant external factors that influenced the way the war was fought. It has been argued that the Americans did not win the war, but the British lost it, "owing the terrain rather than to the enemy."[154] The British were the best military force of the time, fighting linear European-style battles in big, open areas.[155] The mountainous terrain and large regions of wilderness provided an opportunity to offset the main power of the British forces. Knowledge of the area, and understanding of the tactical and strategic implications of the "impenetrable woods and swamps, with no roads or negotiable rivers,"[156] were among the main

---

[154] Laqueur, *Guerrilla Warfare,* 21.

[155] Joes, *America and Guerrilla Warfare,* 12-13.

[156] Laqueur, *Guerrilla Warfare,* 21.

reasons the colonials could fight an effective irregular war.

Another important external factor was the social terrain. Although there was a significant number of British loyalists who fought against the rebels, their suppression by the irregulars and British mismanagement in winning the neutrals' "hearts and minds" led to a significant advantage for the irregulars in popular support.[157] The irregulars got their human resupply from recruits within the local population loyal to the revolutionary cause. The locals often provided food and shelter for the rebel irregulars. Local supporters also warned them of enemy movements and provided vital information about British maneuvers.[158]

Materiel resupply was always a big issue, both for the irregulars and the colonial conventional forces as well. The lack of pre-war established ammunition and weapon stores and an inability to effectively resupply their forces created significant

---

[157] Joes, *America and Guerrilla Warfare,* 39.

[158] Joes, *America and Guerrilla Warfare,* 39-41.

operational difficulties for the rebels. The irregulars got their resupplies mainly from seized British equipment. In many cases, they handed part of their seizures to the conventional army. The irregulars never had enough ammunition. Marion's men "shot with bullets of pewter, buckshot and swan shot. Their swords had been fashioned from saw blades."[159] General Sumter's men sometimes used homemade swords and squirrel rifles instead of muskets, military swords, or bayonets.[160] The rifles, however, provided a significant advantage to the irregulars, since their range and accuracy were superior to the British muskets.

The last important external factor was the American Revolution's alliance with France. This key support occasionally interdicted the most important British supply line due to the French navy's ability to deny the British hegemony on the sea. At key moments, the French prevented the uninterrupted flow of British human and material

[159] Laqueur, *Guerrilla Warfare,* 19.
[160] Joes, *America and Guerrilla Warfare,* 40.

resupplies to the port of the southern coastal cities.[161] This denial significantly contributed to the success of General Greene's integrated strategy, since, as the irregulars exhausted the British in endless chases and inflicted unsustainable numbers of casualties, it became impossible to resupply British troops at the levels needed to continue effective military operations.

F.   CHAPTER   SUMMARY   AND CONCLUSION

The rebel colonies had no standing army before the conflict. Even after the rebel army's quick establishment, its conventional effectiveness was questionable. Although the most significant battles, including Saratoga, Cowpens, Guilford Courthouse and Charleston, were largely fought by regular forces, the commander-in-chief, George Washington admitted that the colonial conventional army, even with the help of the French, was not capable of decisively fighting the British in open,

---

[161] Joes, *America and Guerrilla Warfare,* 21-23.

conventional warfare. It is obvious that if the colonies had chosen to fight a traditional war against their enemy, the British "would have won a complete victory in the summer of 1780."[162] The colonies needed a different strategy to increase their chance of victory. They chose an approach with the primary objective of keeping the revolutionary cause alive. The goal could only be achieved through a strategy that integrated the conventional Continental Army and the irregular forces. There were several key elements that contributed to the success of this approach.

First, the existing militia system, with its mandatory military training, provided an initial force for the colonies to use against the British until the Continental Army was established. Later, the same militia, whose organization, training, and tactics were more suited for guerrilla war than conventional battles, provided a great foundation for the introduction of an irregular strategy. Those

---

[162] Jac Weller, "Irregular but Effective: Partisan Weapons Tactics in the American Revolution: Southern Theatre," *Military Affairs* (Fall 1967), 119.

militia members with experience from previous Indian wars or service in the British colonial army were usually better fighters than those citizens who just signed up to fight for the cause.

Second, the powerful idea of independence and national identity—the American narrative—brought the people of the colonies together and provided strong popular support, which was essential for the success of any irregular forces and operations. This support ensured continuous information superiority and human and material resupply for the rebels, which was a key advantage over the British, who struggled with serious intelligence, manpower, and materiel resupply shortages during the entire war.

Third, the effective military utilization of the physical terrain of North America greatly enhanced the rebels' ability to resist the British forces. The initial advantages of the British were based on their superior numbers, weapons, and training. However, the limited usefulness of British tactics, which were suited to the great European plains, and the limited ability to capitalize on advanced technology, e.g., the new use of artillery units, significantly reduced British superiority. In some cases, their strengths turned into weaknesses and vulnerabilities.

Fourth, the colonials had several leaders who could "think outside of the box" and were willing to seek nontraditional military solutions for their special problems. Nathanael Greene had no previous operational experience; but he was curious about military affairs and had the ability to see things differently. George Washington, Francis Marion, and Thomas Sumter all came from a conventional military background and had experience from previous wars. They were able to capitalize on those experiences and on their knowledge of enemy tactics, techniques and procedures. The mission-oriented task organization of the irregulars, their continuous training, their leaders' ability to turn their strategy's weaknesses to strengths and to ruthlessly exploit the weaknesses of the British, played a key part in the final victory.

Fifth, the symbiotic integration of conventional and irregular forces, which generated local "relative superiority"[163] for the colonial forces led in the end to a strategically overwhelming power. In the south, General Greene took a gamble when he divided his forces, but he knew that General Cornwallis, as conventional thinking would dictate, was eager to destroy or capture both parts of the colonial army to get his "victory." But the more dispersed the British army was, the more exposed each part became to the operations of the irregulars. The result was that "the [British] army was a ship; where it moved in power it commanded, but around it was the hostile sea, parting in front but closing in behind, and always probing for signs of weakness…Whereas a defeated American army could melt back into the countryside from whence it came, a British force so circumscribed was likely to be totally lost."[164]

---

[163] William H. McRaven, *Spec Ops, Case Studies in Special Operations Warfare: Theory and Practice*, (San Marin: Presidio Press, 1995), 4.

[164] Joes, *America and Guerrilla Warfare*, 43.

Sixth, despite the fact that the British and their Tory allies had some sense of irregular tactics from the Seven Years' War and used some of these during the Revolution, they preferred to fight conventionally. As a result, the "not-Christian tactics" used by the colonial irregulars created great confusion, fear, and disorder among the British forces. The British, because of the continuous harassment and shortages in human and material resupply, their inability to effectively tailor their tactics to these challenges, and the increasing number of casualties could not sustain effective military operations.

Seventh, the outside support provided by France was a key element in the rebels' success. The French supply of weapons[165] and money played a significant role in increasing the colonials' military capabilities, but the most important support

---

[165] Nine-tenths of the arms and munitions used by Americans at the Battle of Saratoga were supplied by the French through a cover organization, called Hortalez and Company.

Christopher Felix, *A Short Course in the Secret War*, (New York: Madison Books, 2001), 77.

was provided by the French navy, which at crucial times denied British resupply by sea and blockaded General Cornwallis in Yorktown, preventing his escape and eventually forcing the surrender of his army.

This case serves the purposes of this research well, since analysis of the American Revolutionary War provides several key elements in discovering the validity and exportability of the "professional irregular force" concept as a homeland-defense strategy. At the beginning, there was a not-even-existing, small country, the United States of America, without a standing, conventionally defensive capability. This small country waged a defensive war against a militarily superior occupying force. Even after its hurried establishment of conventional forces, the small country was incapable of fighting on the enemy's terms with any real chance of ultimate success. This small country needed a new approach to take away the foe's advantages. Based on an existing militia, which had training and previous military experience, the small country's forces had a solid irregular organizational and tactical foundation. These abilities were further developed by several key leaders, who took their tactical and operational-level irregular capabilities and combined them into a strategy. The effective employment of the irregular strategy, in combination with some additional factors including favorable terrain and popular and outside support, made it impossible for the superior enemy to effectively answer with a conventional strategy. The struggle between the "indirect" and the "direct" strategies ended in the victory of the small state.

CHAPTER 4
THE BOER WAR

A. BACKGROUND

The origins of this South African War were rooted in a century-old conflict over the domination of Africa south of the Zambezi River, waged between the descendants of mainly Dutch protestant immigrants, called Boers, and the British Empire.[166] The Dutch settlers arrived first in South Africa in the seventeenth century, while the British established their formal rule in Cape Town in 1806. During the Napoleonic Wars, a British expeditionary force landed in Cape Colony and defeated the Dutch defenders, which resulted in the extension of British rule to Cape Colony.[167] During the following decades, British subjects immigrated to the area, slowly matching Boer numbers. With that demographic threat, the Dutch settlers became more and more dissatisfied with the

---

[166] Joes, *Guerrilla Warfare,* 43.

[167] Thomas Pakenham, *The Boer War*, (New York: Random House, 1979), xxi.

British administration and decided to move away from British rule. During the so-called "great trek,"[168] the Boers migrated north towards the interior and established two independent republics: "the Transvaal, with an area of 110,000 square miles containing the cities of Pretoria and Johannesburg, and the Orange Free State, with 49,000 square miles."[169] Though the British initially recognized the two states, their attempted annexation of the Transvaal in 1877 led to the First Boer War, between the Boers and British from 1880 to 1881. After several British defeats, especially that of the Battle of Majuba Hill in 1880, the independence of the Boer republics was restored, but tension remained high.[170]

The discovery of diamonds at Kimberley in 1871 and gold in Transvaal in 1886 resulted in the arrival of massive waves of foreigners, mainly British mine workers. This soon resulted in those

[168] Arquilla, *Insurgents, Raiders and Bandits,* 130.

[169] Joes, *Guerrilla Warfare.* 43.

[170] John P. Wisser, *The Second Boer War. 1899-1900,* (Kansas: Hudson-Kimberly Publishing Company, 1901), 11.

British who searched for jobs and fortune, called "Uitlanders" by the Boers, exceeding the numbers of Boers. In Transvaal, the Boer government saw a serious existential threat from British expansionism in the region and the number of non-Boers. To prevent a possible political takeover by the Uitlanders, the Boer government restricted their voting rights, limited their representation in the administration, and introduced special taxes paid only by them.[171] This discrimination created serious concerns among the Uitlanders, the British government, and even the press, since the *London Times* requested the British administration to stand up more deliberately in support of the Uitlanders.[172]

The escalation of tension led to a small-scale conflict in December 1885, when under the command of Dr. Leander Starr Jameson, "several hundred armed men from British Rhodesia invaded Transvaal"[173] with the hope of igniting a rebellion

[171] Iain R. Smith, *The Origins of the South African War 1890-1902,* (Essex: Longman Group Limited, 1996), 49.

[172] Smith, *The Origins of the South African War 1890-1902,* 98.

among the "Uitlanders" to overthrow the Boer government. The rebellion never happened, and the Boer forces quickly defeated the aggressors. Although the conflict ended in Boer victory, the British did not give up their desire to bring the two Boer republics under their control. This intent and the Uitlander problem caused years of political negotiations to try to reach a compromise. The Boers recognized that if they granted voting rights to the continuously arriving Uitlanders, they would soon become the majority and take away Boers control over the two republics. The negotiation attempts failed, and the British deployed their forces along the borders of Transvaal. In October 1899, the Transvaal government issued an ultimatum stating that "if in 48 hours the British troops did not retire from the border, war existed, and demanded also that the reinforcements already landed, as well as those on the way, be sent back."[174] The British answered that "the conditions imposed by the

---

[173] Joes, *Guerrilla Warfare*. 43.

[174] Wisser, *The Second Boer War. 1899-1900*, 13.

Transvaal were such that the British government could no longer discuss the subject."[175] After the Transvaal government received the reply, it declared war and with the support of its ally, Orange Free State, launched a preemptive invasion against Cape Colony and Natal.[176]

The war consisted of two distinct phases: the conventional phase, from October 1899 to June 1900, and the guerrilla phase, from June 1900 to May 1902.[177] The first phase of the war was based on engagements between conventional armies. The Boers, by exploiting their initial numerical[178] superiority, launched effective strikes into British territory with the operational goal of besieging the British garrisons and isolating important towns, including Mafeking and Kimberley.[179] Although

---

[175] Wisser, *The Second Boer War. 1899-1900*, 13.

[176] Joes, *Guerrilla Warfare*. 44.

[177] Joes, *Guerrilla Warfare*. 44.

[178] The Transvaal had twenty-five thousand men and Orange Free State had an additional fifteen thousand, while the British initially could operate only with ten thousand soldiers.
Joes, *Guerrilla Warfare*. 44.

[179] Wisser, *The Second Boer War. 1899-1900*, 19.

the early period of the war brought numerous victories for the Boers in open battles, including those at Stormberg, Colenso, and Magersfontein, in what was called "Black Week" by the British media,[180] they could not effectively capitalize on these early successes. The Boers wasted their time and resources in hopeless sieges and did not devote the proper effort to invading Cape Colony. This allowed the British to overcome their initial weaknesses, including shortages in reconnaissance and the inability to adjust to local conditions.[181] Furthermore, via sea, the British would eventually send 450,000 troops, "including seventeen thousand Australians and fifty-three thousand white South Africans,"[182] into the conflict within a couple of months. From this moment, the war seemed destined to end in British victory. The British forces quickly relieved the besieged towns and occupied key Transvaal cities, including "Johannesburg in

---

[180] Pakenham, *The Boer War*, 257.

[181] Laqueur, *Guerrilla Warfare,* 89.

[182] Joes, *Guerrilla Warfare.* 44.

May and Pretoria in June 1900."[183] The British believed that the war was close to over with the capture of these two towns, but they were mistaken. The Boer leadership met in March 1900 in Kroonstad and, based on the suggestions of General Christian De Wet, agreed to a next phase and an irregular campaign.[184]

During the second phase of the war, as a response to increasing British strength, the Boers abandoned their previous conventional strategy and introduced irregular warfare to continue fighting. The Boer forces were reorganized into small, mobile units called "commandos" and raided targets such as lines of communications, telegraph stations, railways, and British troop columns. "The Boer columns caused greater damage to the British in this period of the war than ever before. Their incessant maneuvers and frequent attacks exhausted the British forces; their horses died by the thousands."[185]

---

[183] Joes, *Guerrilla Warfare*. 44.

[184] Pakenham, *The Boer War*, 408.

[185] Laqueur, *Guerrilla Warfare,* 90.

To counter the Boers' strategy, the British introduced two key concepts. First, to isolate the commandos from their vital supporters, the population, the British introduced a "scorched-earth" policy. This included the destruction of Boer farms and moving civilians into concentration camps.[186] Second, to curtail the Boer commandos' freedom of movement, the British established the "blockhouse-and-drive system."[187] This concept included a "network of blockhouses at a distance of between eighty and eight-hundred yards, which were connected by barbed wire entanglements, trenches and stone walls,"[188] and large British mounted troops to sweep the area beyond the blockhouses. Finally, the combination of "some hundred-thousand Boer women and children in concentration camps,"[189] continuous attrition, and a British amnesty offer paralyzed the Boer commandos. The Boer forces surrendered 31 May

---

[186] Pakenham, *The Boer War*, 493-495.

[187] Joes, *Guerrilla Warfare*. 45.

[188] Laqueur, *Guerrilla Warfare,* 91.

[189] Laqueur, *Guerrilla Warfare,* 91.

1902. The peace agreement, known as the Treaty of Vereeniging, absorbed the two Boer republics into the British Empire. The agreement included a promise of limited self-governance, which was granted in 1910 with the establishment of the Union of South Africa.

B. IRREGULAR STRATEGY

The Boer republics' military strategy was originally based on conventional positional defense in combination with limited-scale preventive attacks into enemy territory. Although this mindset was deeply rooted in the history of both republics and the Boer culture, the beginning of the war witnessed a certain level of disagreement among political and military leaders about how to fight the British. Some young Boer officers, including Christiaan De Wet and Jan Smuts, recommended the abandonment of the conventional Boer strategy and the introduction of a new approach based on highly mobile "flying commandos."[190] They also

---

[190] The Boers developed this technique in 1838 during

suggested taking the engagements deep into the British colonies and capturing the coastal ports in order to deny the British resupply. On the other hand, the older Boer generals, including the commandant of the Boer forces, Piet Joubert, were in favor of a conventional defensive strategy. This was the reason the first phase of the war was waged in that manner, which caused great Boer losses in materiel, manpower, morale, and, more importantly, opportunities. However this approach brought several initial successes, including Dundee, Colenso, Stormberg, and Magersfontein, though at the same time, it allowed the British to reinforce their troops and launch a large-scale counteroffensive. Jan Smuts explained the reasons behind the failure of this initial strategy when he stated:

---

the war against native Zulu tribes. The Boer soldiers capitalized on their horse-mounted mobility by riding into Zulu territory, dismounting, firing into Zulu formations and fleeing away quickly. This way, one hundred and thirty five Boers defeated approximately twelve thousand Zulus.

Sir Arthur Conan Doyle, *The Great Boer War,* (New York: McClure Phillips and Company, 1902), 6.

> However good the Boers were as raw fighting material, their organization was too loose and ineffective, and their officers too inexperienced and in many glaring cases incompetent, to make a resort to offensive tactics possible. The really capable organizers and leaders in the Boer armies were only slowly coming to the front and many of them had started from the very lowest grades in the organization and were only slowly, and then in spite of gross prejudice and conservative stupidity, moving to more responsible positions ... One of the cardinal mistakes of the Boer plan of campaign was the concentration of all possible forces from all possible parts in defensive positions to stop or delay the advance of the main force of the enemy.[191]

In the light of the failure of their military strategy and the foreseeable fall of the capitals of both countries, the presidents and some senior officers from both republics met in Kroonstad on 17 March 1900 to discuss further actions. Despite the overwhelming number of British forces

---

[191] Rocky Williams, "South African Guerrilla Armies. The Impact of Guerrilla Armies on the Creation of South Africa's Armed Forces," Monograph 127 (2006), accessed November 28, 2011, http://www.iss.co.za/pgcontent.php?UID=18440.

approaching their territory, they decided to continue the war, but under a fundamentally different strategy. The Boer leaders agreed to abandon the extensive use of positional defense along a broad front to prevent the British advance and, based on the suggestions of General Christiaan De Wet, turned the war into a guerrilla campaign. The main goal of De Wet's new strategy was to prolong the war long enough to drain British human and material resources, while hoping for a political backlash in London, which together could have led to a negotiated settlement.

As part of the new approach, the Boer forces were reorganized into small, mounted units, which had to operate in a manner as mobile and self-sufficient as possible. As de Wet explained, "we were of the opinion that we should be able to do better work if we divided the Commandos into small parties. We could not risk any great battles, and, if we divided our forces, the English would have to divide their forces too."[192] These small

---

[192] Christiaan Rudolf De Wet, *Three Years' War*, (New

units focused on attacking and destroying British troop columns and lines of communications and harassing the British forces at every possible place and time.[193] "Commandos became less concerned with occupying ground and permanently seizing positions than with harassing the enemy, overextending their logistical and communication lines and diverting their forces away from the main theatres of operation and the affected civilian populations."[194] This tactically offense-based defensive strategy required the Boers to be masters in the art of maneuver. As General de Wet noted, "to oppose successfully such bodies of men as our burghers had to meet during the war demanded rapidity of action more than anything else. We had to become quick at fighting, quick at reconnoitering, quick, if it became necessary, at flying."[195] Although by this time the British had an

---

York: Charles Scribner's Son, 1985), 225.

[193] André Wessels, "Boer Guerrilla and British Counter-guerrilla Operations in South Africa 1899 to 1902," *Scientia Militaria: South African Journal of Military Studies* 39 (2011), 6.

[194] Williams, "South African Guerrilla Armies."

overwhelming numerical superiority, they had to face the "silent disability of a regular army in contest with a horde of guerrillas maneuvering about their own country. Seldom in the course of the whole campaign in South Africa was it possible for the British Commander-in-Chief or any of his lieutenants, to select their own sites for battle or ground for maneuver."[196]

Although the guerrilla campaign was very successful at the operational and tactical level, the Boer generals and politicians had a hard time maintaining strategic unity. They kept regular communication and all campaigns were first authorized by the political leadership, but "lack of resources, an under-developed politico-military strategy and the dispersed nature of Boer forces led to contradictions, strategic gaps and inconsistencies in the application of this strategy."[197]

---

[195] De Wet, *Three Years' War*, 75.

[196] Maurice Harold Grant, *History of the War in South Africa*, (London: Hurst and Blackett Limited, 1907), 265.

[197] Williams, "South African Guerrilla Armies."

C. ORGANIZATION AND LEADERSHIP

The South African commando system had many similarities with the North American colonial militia. The Boers' citizen-soldier based military service provided a trained defense force in the absence of a regular army. When aggression threatened the Boer republics, the militia was called upon and formed a town-based local commando unit. "All males between sixteen and sixty"[198] were required to serve in the commandos, which usually contained a hundred to a hundred-and-fifty soldiers. The members of the commandos were mostly average farmers bringing their own weapons and horses to the battle. The leaders of these units were elected by the soldiers, but the command system of these units "resembled that of the Boer civilian society, rather loose and uncoordinated, which made effective cooperation and concentration against the enemy more difficult."[199] The commandos were led by a commandant who was

---

[198] Arquilla, *Insurgents, Raiders and Bandits,* 132.
[199] Joes, *Guerrilla Warfare.* 45.

directly responsible to a general, who in theory commanded four commandos. The generals were direct subordinates of the two commanders-in-chief of the Boer republics.

This system was fundamentally transformed at the beginning of the guerrilla phase of the war. "De Wet's strategy called for a major organizational change: the Kommandos were broken into even smaller units than their usual 100 to 150 riders, and were to be widely dispersed."[200] With this new organizational approach, the Boers were able to inflict more damage than during the first phase of the war and to escape repeated British attempts to capture the commandos. The divided units and their maneuvers allowed the Boers "to achieve local superiority long enough to escape"[201] and sometimes were able to trap their pursuers. The self-sufficient elements of these small units could "break into many small groups and travel separately to a new rally point,"[202] where they regrouped and

---

[200] Arquilla, *Insurgents, Raiders and Bandits,* 139.
[201] Arquilla, *Insurgents, Raiders and Bandits,* 140.

attacked their enemies. As Alfred Thayer Mahan, a significant American strategist observed, "Every Boer organization seems susceptible of immediate dissolution into its component units, each of independent vitality, and of subsequent reunion in some assigned place."[203] This new strategy and organizational approach would have not worked with the old generals who had led the Boer units during the first phase of the war and praised the conventional defensive strategy. The irregular phase "found leaders of previously unsuspected guerrilla talents,"[204] including Christiaan Rudolf De Wet and Jan Christiaan Smuts.

Although De Wet's suggestions regarding a new strategic approach were turned down by his superiors at the beginning of the war, he started to employ irregular tactics even in early engagements. In 1899, he played a key role in defeating the British in Natal, at Nicholson's Neck, where his unit

---

[202] Arquilla, *Insurgents, Raiders and Bandits,* 140.

[203] Alfred Thayer Mahan, *The Story of the War in South Africa,* (London: William Clowes, 1900), 203.

[204] Joes, *Guerrilla Warfare.* 45.

outmaneuvered a British force five times its size.
De Wet's commando "took a thousand prisoners,
the largest surrender of British troops in a century."[205]
On another occasion at Sanna's Post, he ambushed
a British column on its flank to draw them in a trap
laid by the rest of his forces along the expected
British retreat line. "The British could not believe
that a poorly educated farmer-turned-soldier of
middle years was capable of such sophistication and
they soon started to spread the false rumor that
Captain Carl Reichmann, the American military
attaché in the field, with De Wet as an observer, had
actually conducted the battle."[206] These victories,
and the British attempts to discredit him, started to
build a personal cult around De Wet. He soon
became a legendary figure, a symbol of Boer
resistance. In his book, *The Great Boer War*, Byron
Farwell argues that after the defeat at Paardeberg, it
was De Wet's personality and actions that kept the

---

[205] Arquilla, *Insurgents, Raiders and Bandits,* 133.
[206] Byron Farwell, *The Great Boer War*, (New York:
Penguin, 1976), 261.

war going.[207] De Wet continuously searched for solutions to mitigate the British numerical superiority and achieve victory. He developed guerrilla warfare and hit-and-run tactics to a level that seemed impossible for the British to cope with. However De Wet never understood why the British designated him and the Boer fighters as guerrillas during the second phase of the war. He believed that the term "guerrilla" could be used only in the case of an occupying force that controls the country from border to border—but this was not the case in any of the Boer republics.[208] De Wet was not just an outstanding strategist and master in the art of maneuvering, but an indefatigable warrior as well, who always fought in the front lines, leading his men by example. He stayed committed to the cause of Boer independence throughout the entire war, even during a personal crisis when his own brother Piet lost his faith in the Boer cause and surrendered to the British. Even after numerous "formal De Wet

---

[207] Farwell, *The Great Boer War*, (New York: Penguin, 1976), 256.

[208] Laqueur, *Guerrilla Warfare,* 92.

hunts," he and his men stayed free to fight until the end of the war.[209] By 1902, as the British soldiered on, De Wet and the Boer forces were "terribly worn hungry and increasingly dispirited,"[210] finally ready for negotiation. The peace offer made by the British, containing a future possibility of self-governance and independence, was good enough even for De Wet, who signed the Treaty of Vereeniging "as president of the Free State" and who in a few years would actually join the government as minister of agriculture.

Like De Wet, other young guerrilla commanders rose during the second phase of the war. One of them was Jan Christiaan Smuts. He came from a perfectly opposite background from De Wet. Smuts was born into a long-established, widely respected traditional Afrikaner family. He was highly educated, having graduated from Cambridge with academic honors. His achievements were later recognized when Lord

---

[209] Arquilla, *Insurgents, Raiders and Bandits,* 141.
[210] Arquilla, *Insurgents, Raiders and Bandits,* 141.

Todd, the Master of Christ's College said in 1970 that "in 500 years of the College's history, of all its members, past and present, three had been truly outstanding: John Milton, Charles Darwin, and Jan Smuts."[211] In 1895, Smuts became a personal legal advisor for Cecil Rhodes and, with that, a target for the Boer press, which saw their archenemy in Rhodes. After the Jameson raid, he felt betrayed by his employer and resigned immediately. Smuts moved to Pretoria and soon became a committed supporter of the Transvaal president, Paul Kruger. As a reward for his services, in June 1898, Kruger appointed Smuts as state attorney. At the beginning of the war, Smuts was responsible for handling international communication, propaganda, and strategic-level logistics as well. His career as a significant irregular leader started during the second phase, when he served as an officer under the command of Koos de la Rey.

Like De Wet, Smuts proved to have

---

[211]Jan Smuts, *Memoirs of the Boer War*, (London: Jonathan Ball Publishers, 1997), xi.

excellent capabilities in adopting and further developing hit-and-run tactics and generally outmaneuvering British columns. He proved himself not only a master planner, but also a brave soldier and intelligent leader who was aware of the capabilities and limitations of his men. During operations, his forces not only ambushed British columns and attacked supply lines, but spread Boer propaganda to ignite additional revolts against the British and intimidate those who opposed the Boer cause. When the British introduced the scorched-earth policy, combined with a network of blockhouses and flying sweeps, Smuts himself evaded them at least a dozen times. Once he led five-hundred men out of a trap established by twenty-thousand British troops.[212]

These abilities were the reason why Smuts was chosen by his superiors for a mission that they hoped would turn the war in favor of the Boers. Smuts led 340 men on a raid into the heart of the British Cape Colony with the overall goal of

---

[212] Smuts, *Memoirs of the Boer War*, 19-25.

igniting a general uprising against the British. By the time his widely spread and stealthily moving force met again after a month on the border, he had only 240 men left.[213] Also, when they made it to Cape Colony, Smuts and his forces were deep in enemy territory and cut off from any resupply. His men, weakened by the continuous evasion, starvation, and disease, soon turned against Smuts, but he managed to keep their motivation and belief in the cause high. Their luck finally turned when, during a raid on a British cavalry unit, they took horses, clothes, food and ammunition, which gave their self-belief back.

Although Smuts and his commandos were successful at harassing the British in their own territory, they initially could not achieve their ultimate goal. After Smuts realized that his small-scale raids were not going to ignite the rebellion, he decided to establish a command post and start acting as the leader of an entire army to attract the local Boers. He implemented his raiding strategy

---

[213] Smuts, *Memoirs of the Boer War*, 139-155.

with propaganda and recruiting activity, and as a result his force soon numbered 3,000 fighters. Witnessing Smuts's success, the British commander, General Kitchener noted, "the dark days are on us again." Smuts himself wrote about the results of his operations, "We practically held the whole area from the Olifants to the Orange river 400 miles away, save for small garrison towns here and there."[214] After assessing the situation, he decided to take the initiative once again and launch an attack to bring the British to the negotiating table.

Using all his forces, he launched an attack against the copper mining of Okiep. Although his forces could surround the town, he could not launch a direct attack on the fortified British garrison. Once again, Smuts proved his abilities in irregular thinking. Instead of a conventional siege, he packed a train with explosives and planned to detonate it in the town near the garrison. Although this attempt

---

[214] Deneys Reitz and J. C. Smuts, *Commando: A Boer Journal of the Boer War*, (London: Faber and Faber Limited, 1929), 310.

failed, the British soon offered him a peace conference to discuss the conditions of a possible peace agreement.[215] Although his operation never really achieved its original goal, it still had a significant influence on the future military thinking of the British, playing a key role in the concept of the establishment of the British commandos and other special forces.

D. INTERNAL FACTORS

When not at war, the average Boer fighters were farmers who were working in their fields every day. To get meat, they pretty much depended on their weapon and horse. Hunting was not only a source of food, but a significant developer of individual skills. They learned how to shoot from different positions, including the prone position, as well as how to use cover and concealment. As hunters, the Boers also learned the importance of aimed shooting, since if they missed the first shot, the game would escape. They further developed

---

[215] Reitz, *Commando,* 298-305.

their marksmanship during social gatherings, when shooting competitions were major events. They used smokeless gunpowder, which later made it very hard for the British to track them, since they could not identify their positions. During hunting, the Boers developed the ability to live in the field and sustain themselves for a long time without resupply. Their other significant capability was riding skill. Based on the individual Boer fighters' riding capabilities and experiences from previous wars against the Zulus,[216] the commandos became experts in light-cavalry operations.

Using all these skills, the Boer units could take the classical hit-and-run tactic to the next level. The commandos operated behind British lines, penetrating deep into enemy territory, where they ambushed convoys, destroyed railroads, cut communication lines, and attacked the British forces from the flank and rear. "There was no convoy whose safe arrival could be counted on, not a garrison that did not stand continually to arms, not

---

[216] Arquilla, *Insurgents, Raiders and Bandits,* 130.

a column which even whilst it marched against the enemy had not to move with the strictest precautions of the defensive."[217] The commandos' tactics "relied on mobility to repeatedly effectuate surprise, after which they would withdraw again as soon as possible to minimize the risk of suffering casualties."[218] The Boers' "use of mobility and maneuver was to impress generations of military officers and to concretely influence the development of doctrines for mobile and maneuver warfare in the armed forces of Europe."[219]At the same time, as Smuts' operations showed, the Boers were also expert in using propaganda to their advantage while suppressing any voice who opposed them. The commando success initially was also based on information advantages. The supportive local population and the Boer reliance on mounted reconnaissance patrols provided a reliable intelligence system for the commandos. Conversely,

[217] Grant, *History of the War in South Africa*, 397.

[218] Wessels, "Boer Guerrilla and British Counter-guerrilla Operations in South Africa," 7.

[219] Williams, "South African Guerrilla Armies."

there was serious British negligence regarding intelligence, which added to the existing operational advantages held by the Boers. These factors led to victories, such as De Wet's at Mostert's Hoek, where his commando killed fifty British soldiers and captured the rest of the force.[220] This situation changed when the British overcame their shortages on reconnaissance and when around two thousand Boers, who convinced themselves that any further resistance was hopeless, joined the British against their own people as National Scouts.[221]

The success of Boer tactics was significant, because like the irregulars of the American Revolutionary War, there was no formal doctrine codifying the activities of the Boer commandos. No effort other than some initial attempts by the Transvaal artillery officers to develop their own doctrine was made to put the Boer way of fighting into manuals. As an irregular phenomenon, the tactics used by the Boer fighters were based more

---

[220] Arquilla, *Insurgents, Raiders and Bandits,* 136.

[221] Joes, *Guerrilla Warfare.* 45.

on their individual skills and previous war experiences than anything else "learned in a formal military environment."[222] Paul Johnston captured this point in his article, "Doctrine is Not Enough: The Effect of Doctrine on the Behavior of Armies," "ultimately, an army's behavior in battle will almost certainly be more of a reflection of its character or culture than of the contents of its doctrine manuals. And if that culture—or mind set, if you will—is formed more by experience than by books, then those who would attempt to modify an army's behavior need to think beyond doctrine manuals."[223]

E. EXTERNAL FACTORS

The commandos were extensively deployed in their own areas where the Boer fighters had detailed knowledge of the local terrain. As Anthony James Joes explained, the "vast stretches of the Boer republics were level and treeless, excellent

---

[222] Williams, "South African Guerrilla Armies."

[223] Paul Johnston, "Doctrine is not enough: The Effect of Doctrine on the Behavior of Armies," *Parameters*: US Army War College Quarterly, 2000, 37.

territory for mounted guerrillas in the pre-aircraft age."[224] The Boer leaders could effectively suit the Boers' traditional mounted warfare to the terrain of the two republics. Although about 20,000 Boers remained free to fight towards the end of the conflict, the British blockhouse network and the introduction of mounted "quick-reaction forces" managed to severely restrict the Boers' ability to exploit the terrain, taking away their initial operational advantage.

Knowledge of the terrain was not the only advantage the commandos had when fighting in their well-known home areas. The other significant advantage was the personal relationship of the fighters with the local population. As in any classic guerrilla struggle, the population played a key role in the Second Boer War. They provided food, shelter, and information to the commandos, which gave them an initial information advantage over the British. They also provided manpower for the Boer cause. It happened many times that even those

---

[224] Joes, *Guerrilla Warfare.* 45.

Boers who earlier surrendered or made an agreement with the British volunteered again to fight. Examples include De Wet's victory at Mostert's Hock, where he re-recruited some men from Reddersburg "who had just weeks before accepted Roberts' amnesty offer"[225] and Smuts' raid where he was able to recruit about 3,000 men behind enemy lines to fight for the cause. The importance of the civilian population in this conflict was quickly recognized by the British. To isolate the commandos from the population and to deny them information, food, and manpower the British established concentration camps when they introduced the earlier mentioned scorched-earth policy.[226] In the camps, malaria, pneumonia, bronchitis, and typhoid fever caused 3,165 civilian deaths within a single month in 1901.[227] During the two-year guerrilla phase of the war, conditions in the concentration camps killed approximately

---

[225] Arquilla, *Insurgents, Raiders and Bandits,* 136.

[226] Joes, *Guerrilla Warfare.* 46.

[227] Denis Judd and Keith Surridge, *The Boer War,* (New York: Palgrave MacMillan, 2003), 194.

25,000 civilians.[228] Although the suffering of mostly women and children in the camps and the ever-increasing problem of food shortages had a significant effect on the morale of the commandos, it also seemed to help Boer propaganda, since British actions created an outrage in London. "Henry Campbell-Bannerman, leader of the opposition Liberal party, declared that the British forces were employing methods of barbarism."[229] Emily Hobhouse, the leader of the South African Women and Children's Distress Fund and of the "Ladies Committee," brought world attention to the suffering of people in the camps and also to the atrocities conducted by the British troops in South Africa. Her activity created a widespread public criticism of the government and put great pressure on the authorities to relieve the British commander, General Kitchener. [230] These events served well the Boers' strategy, as it aimed for victory through

---

[228] Surridge, *The Boer War,* 194.

[229] Joes, *Guerrilla Warfare.* 46.

[230] Arquilla, *Insurgents, Raiders and Bandits,* 139.

British exhaustion and internal social conflict. To capitalize on this opportunity and extend their "psychological operations" abroad, Boer leaders sent out several politicians to gain international support. This was important since, other than some moral support from the Netherlands and Germany, the Boer republics had no international support against the British. "A. Fischer, C.H. Wessels and A.D.W. Wolmarans visited the Netherlands and the United States as well as France, Germany, and Russia, but without achieving success"[231] and no real material support was given to the Boers.

F. CHAPTER SUMMARY AND CONCLUSION

Although the Boer republics had no standing army or written doctrine before the conflict, the commando members' individual skills and prior war experiences made them an effective fighting force, especially during the guerrilla phase. They possessed tactical advantages over the British even

[231] Wessels, "Boer Guerrilla and British Counter-guerrilla Operations in South Africa," 10.

towards the end of the conflict. "In tactical engagements they continued to hold the advantage in mobility, being all mounted, as well as in marksmanship at ranges up to and beyond a mile. The smokeless powder they used made it hard for the British to track them, even when they were enclosed in set traps."[232] The Boer commandos used numerous irregular warfare elements, including guerrilla warfare and psychological operations during the war, but these efforts were not enough to achieve a final victory. There are several key conditions that contributed to the failure of the Boers' irregular strategy.

The initial disagreement among the Boer leaders about how to fight the British led to a situation at the beginning of the war where, in Arreguín-Toft's words, two similar strategies met and led to the stronger side's victory. Although at the beginning of the conflict Boer forces held a numerical advantage, they wasted their time, manpower, and material resources trying to fight the

---

[232] Arquilla, *Insurgents, Raiders and Bandits,* 140.

British conventionally in open battles and siege operations. Despite their initial tactical-level successes, this strategy had a major negative impact, since the Boers tried to wage a kind of war for which their forces were not designed and their fighters were not trained. They did not have siege equipment and, as Thomas Pakenham noted, "indeed, the commando system was best suited not to large-scale set-piece battles, but to smaller-scale, guerrilla strikes."[233] It is clear that during the initial phase of the war, the Boers failed to capitalize on their biggest strength, which allowed the British to use their command of the sea to quickly reinforce their forces and gain numerical superiority. This changed the course of the war, and the Boers needed to change their strategy to continue the fight.

The new approach would have required a key condition to be successful: national integrity. After the catastrophic defeat at Paardeberg, many Boers decided that the struggle was hopeless. The

---

[233]Pakenham, *The Boer War*, 348.

number of surrendering Boers continuously increased through time, due to the combination of harsh British tactics and amnesty offers. The loss of manpower and the difficulty in recruiting new fighters caused a huge setback for the Boer irregular strategy—as did the approximately 2,000 Boers who volunteered to fight against their own brothers as British scouts. This eroded not just national integrity, but one of the most important advantages of the guerrillas, their one-sided exploitation of the terrain.

Another key condition that led to the failure of the strategy was that the Boer decision to wage a guerrilla war was an ad-hoc one in the wake of conventional defeat. The lack of a previously existing national-level irregular strategy led to a series of military operations without an integrated political–military goal. The Boer forces' main purpose was to harass the British and to inflict as many casualties as possible, with the hope that they would become exhausted and be forced to the negotiation table. Although the commandos were very effective at the tactical level, their individual unit successes were not enough to bring the final victory.

As part of the ad hoc application of irregular warfare, the Boers also failed to establish proper information and resupply networks. Those that existed were based on the local populations and their farms. With the introduction of harsh British methods, including concentration camps and scorched earth, these systems were almost entirely neutralized. This lack of supporting infrastructure and the British ability to tailor their tactics to the special requirements of the conflict, including the blockhouse network and sweeping drives, seriously limited the Boer guerrillas' freedom of movement. This was further restricted by the lack of any safe havens abroad.[234]

Last, but not least, the new tactics introduced by the British created some criticism in London and around the world, but the British political and military strategy was never

---

[234] Joes, *Guerrilla Warfare.* 46.

undermined sufficiently to affect the outcome of the conflict. The Boers failed not just in convincing the British voters about their cause, but in gaining significant outside support from other countries. This failure was reinforced by the fact that, unlike the situation during the American Revolutionary War, Great Britain was not engaged in any other war and there was no other country yet challenging its sea hegemony.[235] The Boers were left on their own to fight a superior enemy and could not turn the odds to their favor.

This case was chosen as a subject of analysis because it carries numerous learning points for those who are looking at the validity of an irregular warfare-based defensive strategy. The organization, equipment, and training of the Boer republics' defensive forces were better tailored to irregular warfare than conventional war and for defensive goals than offensive. However, at the beginning of the war, the political and military leadership of the

---

[235] The great Anglo-German naval arms race to build dreadnought battleships did not begin until the year after the Boer War ended.

countries decided to fight traditionally and to attack the British. During the first phase of the war, an already existing irregular force and its resources were wasted. When the Boer leadership realized its mistake, it was too late to turn events around. The effective tactical-level irregular warfare demonstrated by the Boers during the second phase of the war "still resonates loudly among all those today who think about or are called upon to fight irregular wars;"[236] but this case shows that some of the key requirements for success identified in the previous case study—including high-level individual training, knowledge of local terrain, mobility, and expertise in irregular warfare—by themselves do not guarantee final victory. The lack of an effective national-level, integrated irregular strategy, the inability to gain any external support, and the enemy's ability to focus all its effort towards the Boers led to a situation where the struggle of the "indirect" and the "direct" strategies ended with the victory of the large state. But if the

---

[236] Arquilla, *Insurgents, Raiders and Bandits,* 140.

Boers had begun with an irregular warfare approach, and adhered to it, British prospects for ultimate victory would have been poor.

CHAPTER 5
THE WAR IN GERMAN EAST AFRICA

A. BACKGROUND

Germany, as a late arrival in the "scramble for Africa," had only four areas left to colonize: "Togo, Cameroon, South-West Africa and East Africa."[237] Among these colonies, East Africa quickly became "the jewel of the German Colonial Empire."[238] However Germany's appearance in Africa further deepened the existing tensions among the colonial powers. They seemed to have "a common desire to develop (or exploit) rather than fight over (and devastate) their African colonies, and a common determination to safeguard racial 'prestige', had fostered increasing rapprochement among the colonial powers."[239] The basis for this common agreement was provided by the Congo Act, signed by the colonial powers in 1885. They

---

[237] Arquilla, *Insurgents, Raiders and Bandits,* 144.

[238] Brian Gardner, *German East. The Story of the First World War in East Africa*, (London: Cassell and Company ltd., 1963), 7.

[239] Edward Paice, *Tip and Run. The Untold Tragedy of the Great War in Africa*, (London: Phoenix, 2008), 2.

agreed not to take war to Africa "in the event of an outbreak of conflict in Europe."[240]

At the beginning of the First World War, colonial leaders on both sides believed, based on the Congo Act that the conflict would not be taken to Africa. The governor of German East Africa, Heinrich Schnee "was not interested in war."[241] He ordered the commander-in-chief of German East Africa, Colonel Paul Emil von Lettow-Vorbeck, whose plans for defending the colony Schnee was not even willing to hear, not to take any hostile actions.[242] At the same time, the British colonial governor, Henry Conway Belfield, also stated that "this colony had no interest in the present war."[243] But this mindset changed very quickly as the British higher command identified the "wireless stations and ports of Germany's African colonies"[244] as a

---

[240] Arquilla, *Insurgents, Raiders and Bandits*, 145.

[241] Gardner, *German East*, 10.

[242] Charles Miller, *Battle for the Bundu: The First World War in East Africa*, (New York: MacMillan Publishing Co., Inc. 1974), 41.

[243] Byron Farwell, *The Great War in Africa, 1914–1918*, (New York: W.W. Norton & Company, 1989), 122.

threat to British shipping lanes and its strategy called for land war against the German defense forces in Africa.

Since Dar-es-Salaam, the capital of German East Africa, had a wireless station, the war soon arrived there as well. On August 8, 1914 two British cruisers, the *Astraea* and the *Pegasus* started to shell Dar-es-Salaam with the primary goal of destroying the city's wireless tower. From the same ships, a small unit of British marines landed in the city and, with the support of the German governor, a truce was signed with the locals not to engage in any hostile act against the British during the war. [245] This agreement further undermined the relationship between Governor Schnee and Von Lettow, as the latter saw that the war in Africa could play a key role in the success of the fatherland back in Europe. In his book, called *My Reminiscences of East*

---

[244] Paice, *Tip and Run*, 3.

[245] Paul Emil Von Lettow-Vorbeck, *My Reminiscences of East Africa*, (Uckfield: The Naval and Military Press ltd.), 28-29.

Africa, Von Lettow explained his point of view by saying:

> The question was whether it was possible for us in our subsidiary theatre of war to exercise any influence on the great decision at home. Could we, with our small forces, prevent considerable numbers of the enemy from intervening in Europe, or in other more important theatres, or inflict on our enemies any loss of personnel or war material worth mentioning.[246]

He understood that he could only achieve this goal by mounting an effective defense in the colony. Von Lettow formulated a strategy along this objective, his available forces, and the size of his area of operations.

The German colonial forces, called *Schutztruppe,* initially consisted of about 250 German officers and a little more than 2,500 Askari fighters.[247] These forces were supposed to defend a colony as large as Germany and France combined

---

[246] Von Lettow-Vorbeck, *My Reminiscences of East Africa*, 3.

[247] Arquilla, *Insurgents, Raiders and Bandits*, 146.

and encompassed the present-day Tanzania, Rwanda, and Burundi.[248] Further, German East Africa "was surrounded by colonies of Allied powers: Britain's East Africa (mostly today's Kenya), Rhodesia, and Nyasaland; the Belgian Congo;"[249] and Mozambique.[250] However, the Allied powers, initially having only seventeen companies of African troops in their disposal,[251] did not have significant numerical advantages over the German forces. But the Royal Navy's command of the sea allowed the British to introduce more troops to the theater swiftly and the navy also "completed the envelopment of the seemingly helpless German colony."[252] Based on these facts, the British were certain that the land war in Africa "would be little more than a short, sharp affair

---

[248] Paice, *Tip and Run*, 3-4.

[249] Arquilla, *Insurgents, Raiders and Bandits*, 147.

[250] Mozambique was significant only after 1916 when Portugal decided to join the war on the British side. Arquilla, *Insurgents, Raiders and Bandits*, 147.

[251] Gardner, *German East*, 10.

[252] Arquilla, *Insurgents, Raiders and Bandits*, 148.

concluded by Christmas 1914,"[253] but Von Lettow had a different opinion.

Realizing that any conventional approach to defending the colony was not possible, Von Lettow introduced a unique defensive strategy. Instead of massing his forces, he broke them into small units and dispersed them along the borders of the colony and in the key coastal towns. According to his approach, these small elements could do two things. First, starting in the fall of 1914, they could conduct harassing operations against British outposts and troop columns. Second, in case of a British offensive, these small units could fight a holding action long enough to allow the other closely located units to swarm around the enemy and come to their aid. This approach soon proved its effectiveness when the British staged an amphibious assault against Tanga in November 1914. The attacking force, about 8,000 Indian troops with naval support under the command of Major General Arthur Edward Aitken, faced just 200

---

[253] Paice, *Tip and Run*, 3.

Germans and Askaris, whose initial holding allowed Von Lettow to bring in reinforcement and forced the British to retreat. The British *Official History of the War* describes the events at Tanga as one of "the most notable failures in British military history."[254]

Shortly after their failure at Tanga, the British tried to launch an attack again from the sea with the goal of occupying Dar-es-Salaam. The Royal Navy bombarded the city, but the defenders "returned a fierce and accurate fire, inflicting damage on a number of British vessels."[255] The British realized that the invasion of the city would possibly end with similar results as the operation at Tanga, and decided to withdraw from the shores of the capital. In November 1914, the British cabinet decided that the "control of operations in East Africa was to be taken over by the War Office"[256] and General Aitken was replaced by Major General Richards Wapshare.

---

[254] Farwell, *The Great War in Africa*, 178.

[255] Arquilla, *Insurgents, Raiders and Bandits*, 150.

[256] Gardner, *German East*, 41.

During the last days of 1914, the British launched a land offensive from the north and temporarily occupied a town called Jasin; but Von Lettow's units arrived to help their peers and by mid-January, forced the British to withdraw again. "The British casualties were nearly 500. Says the official history. "The morale of the British forces undoubtedly had again been shaken and they were not likely to be capable of passing to the offensive for some time to come."[257] After the battle at Jasin, Von Lettow took over the initiative from the British. He ordered his forces to be even more subdivided and start conducting near-constant raids against the British, especially targeting the British East Africa railroad. The German units conducted so many operations that the British believed that Von Lettow's army was much larger than its actual size. These operations proved to be so successful that the War Office ordered the British forces "to stand on the defensive and try to hold on to what they already had."[258] At the same time, the British

---

[257] Gardner, *German East*, 43.

high command and the commander-in-chief, General Kitchener, realized that they would have to deal with the German force decisively in Africa. To be able to do so, they reasoned that they needed to send in a much larger force to defeat Von Lettow.

The New Year brought significant changes in the course of the war. Large numbers of fresh British units arrived in Africa led by an "energetic new commander: the Boer-hero-turned-British-loyalist, Jan Smuts"[259] who brought a significant number of experienced Boers with him. To cope with the new threat, a multidirectional attack, Von Lettow immediately changed his approach and started to focus on strategic defense once again. He did not send out his small forces on raids anymore, but went back to his initial strategy. The concept was to hold up the enemy as long as possible while causing maximum damage, and then withdrawing before being outflanked. The strategy seemed to be working with varying effectiveness against different

---

[258] Arquilla, *Insurgents, Raiders and Bandits*, 150.
[259] Arquilla, *Insurgents, Raiders and Bandits*, 151.

enemies. While it could completely stop the advance of the Portuguese, in the case of the Boer units, it only slowed their maneuvers and increased their casualties. The fighting continued "week after week, month after month."[260]

Throughout the next two years, the British kept pushing Von Lettow southward. He "resisted, falling back slowly, inflicting as much damage as he could and delaying the seemingly inevitable loss of the colony for as long as possible."[261] At this time, he also had to "fight" with Governor Schnee as well, who called for a surrender, but Von Lettow ignored his civilian superior's request. In October 1917, the British commander Major General Jacobus van Deventer[262] thought that the German forces were close to the end and only one more push was needed to destroy them. At the Mahiwa River, Van Deventer attacked Von Lettow's forces with

---

[260] Arquilla, *Insurgents, Raiders and Bandits*, 151.

[261] Arquilla, *Insurgents, Raiders and Bandits*, 152.

[262] He replaced General Smuts when the latter was called to Britain at the end of 1916 to serve on the Imperial War Council.

Arquilla, *Insurgents, Raiders and Bandits*, 152.

about 6,000 troops. By contrast with the previous operational pattern, this time the Germans decided to stay and fight. The several-days'-long battle ended with Von Lettow's victory, but he paid a high price for it by losing about a third of his forces. The British thought that they had finally beaten Von Lettow, but he again shifted his strategy and mounted a strategic offense.

The German forces initially moved away from the enemy by invading Portugal's Mozambique colony. There they gained sufficient supplies and ammunition by defeating a 1,500-man-strong Portuguese unit. With pursuers on his tail, Von Lettow continued his offensive in Mozambique during the next nine months. Eventually he decided to move back into German East Africa and reentered the colony with his troops. There he attacked British depots and small-unit columns, and started to return his force closely to complete fitness.[263] "Von Lettow kept up the pressure right until the end of the war in November 1918."[264] On

---

[263] Gardner, *German East*, 187.

13 November 1918, two days after the Armistice was signed in France, when encamped with his forces at the Chambezi River, Lettow-Vorbeck was handed a telegram by a British messenger stating that the war was over. After two days of thinking and trying to confirm the news, Von Lettow finally agreed to surrender, and as General Van Deventer requested, he led his undefeated forces to Abercorn and formally surrendered on 23 November 1918.[265]

B. IRREGULAR STRATEGY

By looking at the geographical location, the size of the area he wanted to defend, and the limited number of his forces, Von Lettow quickly understood that the classical German strategy, which was followed by Frederick the Great during the Seven Years' War,[266] would not work in

---

[264] Arquilla, *Insurgents, Raiders and Bandits*, 154.

[265] Gardner, *German East*, 190-191.

[266] During the Seven Years' War between 1756 and 1763, Frederick the Great attacked the invading French, Austrian and Russian forces from his central positions when he kept his forces massed.

Arquilla, *Insurgents, Raiders and Bandits*, 148.

German East Africa. He realized that it was impossible to defend the colony by following conventional strategy, since it was threatened from the land and from the sea. "The Colony could not be ensured even by purely defensive tactics, since the total length of land frontier and coast-line was about equal to that of Germany."[267]

This conclusion was further reinforced by the fact that his communication was almost completely cut with the fatherland from the beginning of the war, and that because of the high demands of the European theater and the great risk posed by the Royal Navy, the colonial forces could not expect any reinforcement. Von Lettow, based on his experiences gained during the counterinsurgent campaigns between 1904 and 1905 against the rebellious Herero and Nama tribes in South-West Africa, and also from interacting with Boer veterans while he was in South Africa to

---

[267] Von Lettow-Vorbeck, *My Reminiscences of East Africa*, 4.

receive medical treatment,[268] came up with an irregular approach.

He took his conventionally organized and trained forces and turned them into an irregular force. At the beginning of the conflict, Von Lettow broke his forces into small, company-size elements containing 100 to 150 Askaris and several German officers and created a network of defense nests by placing them in the key ports and along the frontiers of the colony. "The idea was that each small detachment could fight an initial holding action when it came under attack; other nearby companies of *Schutztruppe* would then come in support as needed. They would be like the antibodies of the human immune system."[269] This system proved its effectiveness both in the ports and inland. At the battle of Tanga, the British amphibious force, though eight times larger than the defenders, was forced to withdraw. In another case, the town of Jasin was temporarily taken by the British, but

---

[268] Arquilla, *Insurgents, Raiders and Bandits*, 144-145.
[269] Arquilla, *Insurgents, Raiders and Bandits*, 148.

"swarming"[270] German units quickly drove them off and retook the town. These company-size units proved their effectiveness, but they also sustained high casualties and lost a large amount of materiel. One seventh of the original officer corps died and as Von Lettow stated, "the expenditure of 200,000 rounds also proved that with the means at my disposal I could at the most fight three more actions of this nature."[271] Von Lettow realized that his forces could not sustain such losses in a long war as they had during their initial operations and that he needed to rethink his approach to economize his forces for a long war.

Von Lettow explained "the need to strike great blows only quite exceptionally, and to restrict myself principally to guerrilla warfare, was

---

[270] The phenomenon, as John Arquilla and David Ronfeldt defined it, is the systematic pulsing of force and/or fire by dispersed units, so as to strike the adversary from all directions simultaneously.

John Arquilla and David Ronfeldt. *Swarming & the Future of Conflict*, (Santa Monica: RAND Coorporation, 2000), 8

[271] Von Lettow-Vorbeck, *My Reminiscences of East Africa*, 63.

evidently imperative."[272] Based on this view, he subdivided his units even further, into detachments of eight to ten men, Europeans and Askaris, in order to conduct raids behind enemy lines. These small units "rode round the rear of the enemy's camps, which had been pushed up as far as the Longido, and attacked their communications."[273] Since Von Lettow's swarming units appeared in so many places and they "went farther and deeper, creating increasingly annoying disruptions,"[274] they actually made the British believe that they were facing a much larger enemy then they really were. Through his irregular strategy, Von Lettow forced the British to assume a defensive posture and stay there for almost the entire year of 1915, which allowed him to keep the initiative throughout this period. But the beginning of 1916 brought fundamental changes in the British strategy.

---

[272] Von Lettow-Vorbeck, *My Reminiscences of East Africa*, 63.

[273] Von Lettow-Vorbeck, *My Reminiscences of East Africa*, 64.

[274] Arquilla, *Insurgents, Raiders and Bandits*, 150.

The introduction of a large number of fresh British troops, the Portuguese decision to join the war, and the appointment of General Smuts to command the British forces forced Von Lettow to think through his strategy again. He was able to adapt to the changed situation once more and went back to his original concept. He reorganized his forces once again into company-sized units and dispersed them in the same manner as at the beginning of the war. The concept was the same as in 1914; the companies were to fight holding actions as long as practicable, than withdraw when necessary. Although at that time the loss of the colony seemed inevitable, through this irregular approach Von Lettow and his forces were able to fight an enemy, which by that time had become numerically and technologically far superior, for an additional two years. Towards the end of 1917, Von Lettow's handful of soldiers was chased by about 150,000 Allied troops, who were supported by nearly a quarter-million African porters.[275] By this

---

[275] Paice, *Tip and Run*, 3.

time, the British thought that they finally cornered the German forces, but Von Lettow proved his genius in irregular operations. Instead of fighting a positional defense, he switched to the strategic offensive. He maneuvered his forces into Mozambique, moving away from the main enemy forces and gaining supplies from defeated small enemy detachments. Throughout the next year, his pursuers could not catch Von Lettow, who even managed to refit his forces almost to their original level; and in the fall of 1918, he shifted his offensive back to German East Africa. The British thought many times during the war that they were close to defeating Von Lettow and his forces, but the *Schutztruppe* kept conducting effective operations until the last day of the war.[276]

C. ORGANIZATION AND LEADERSHIP

Von Lettow's forces started the war with their organization designed for conventional war. The defense forces "consisted of 216 Europeans and

---

[276] Gardner, *German East*, 154.

2,540 Askari."[277] In addition to that, there were two ships available, "the company of the *Königsberg*, 322 men, and of the *Möwe*, 102 men."[278] The organizational framework of the East German colonial land forces was the company. The available troops were organized into fourteen companies, each of them consisting of 160 men organized into three platoons of 50 troops, including two machine-gun teams. Every company had 250 carriers attached as well as several native fighters, called Ruga-Ruga.[279] Each of these companies was named after its garrison's location. During the war, the number of these units varied from fifteen to 30. In addition to the original companies, some *Schützenkompagnies* or rifle companies, were organized as well, which initially consisted of only white settlers, but as the conflict progressed, became racially mixed. The total number of the companies never exceeded 60.[280] The size of these

---

[277] Gardner, *German East*, 10.

[278] Von Lettow-Vorbeck, *My Reminiscences of East Africa*, 19.

[279] Miller, *Battle for the Bundu*, 18.

units greatly varied through the war, based on the number of casualties suffered and recruits gained.

His initial conventional company organization served Von Lettow's irregular defensive strategy well. These were cohesive units, mostly trained to fight only at the company level, and that was what Von Lettow initially needed the most. He stated that "it was impossible to employ them in large formations, or to train the senior officers in this respect. It was evident that in war the movement and leading in battle of forces greater than a company would be attended with great difficulty and friction."[281] However, the companies suited the initial concept of operation, of one company conducting holding actions with others swarming around the enemy as needed or conducting raids against the British in their own territory. But the relatively heavy losses both in human lives and materiel, forced Von Lettow to

---

[280] Von Lettow-Vorbeck, *My Reminiscences of East Africa*, 71.

[281] Von Lettow-Vorbeck, *My Reminiscences of East Africa*, 9.

rethink his strategy at the beginning of 1915.

Nevertheless, the guiding principle of his approach remained to mount an effective defense while constantly sustaining raids in the British territories. "It was in any case impossible to act with larger forces."[282] The restrictions imposed by the terrain also required a shift in the organization of the German forces. "A company even was too large a force to send across this desert, and if, after several days of marching, it really had reached some point on the railway, it would have had to come back again, because it could not be supplied."[283] In order to meet his objectives, Von Lettow further subdivided his forces and created a large number of small, eight-to-ten-man detachments containing Europeans and Askaris. These units were able to move fast and light and caused great damage behind enemy lines. These operations served multiple purposes: they gathered information about the

---

[282] Von Lettow-Vorbeck, *My Reminiscences of East Africa*, 64.

[283] Von Lettow-Vorbeck, *My Reminiscences of East Africa*, 64.

enemy, seized supplies, and inflicted as many casualties as they could. As a result of their effectiveness, the British assumed a defensive posture and remained in it throughout 1915. The introduction of a large number of Allied troops at the beginning of 1916 forced the Germans to go back to their original company-based organization, which they used during the rest of the war.

The impossible-looking challenge of defending the colony, and the limitations created by the initial setup of the defense forces of German East Africa, required a leader with exceptional abilities. And while the Germans needed all of their experienced commanders back in Europe, they decided to send "The German army's most experienced colonial warfare officer,"[284] Paul Emil Von Lettow-Vorbeck to prepare the defense of the colony. As his actions later proved, he was the right man for the job. Von Lettow's experience came from counterinsurgent operations in China during the Boxer Rebellion in 1900 and in South-West Africa

---

[284] Arquilla, *Insurgents, Raiders and Bandits*, 146.

against the Herero and the Nama tribes in 1904–
1905. From 1909 to 1913, he was also in charge of
a German marine unit, "the closet thing the
Germans had at the time to troops ready to fight in
irregular settings."[285] Brian Gardner, in his book
*German East, The Story of the First World War in
East Africa*, noted about Von Lettow that "by 1914
he had enjoyed a more varied experience than
probably any other German officer, having taken
part in naval maneuvers in large and small ships,
bush fighting, combat in China and a great deal of
mixed staff and regimental duties."[286] These
experiences allowed him to be able to think not only
conventionally, but, when the situation required, in
irregular terms as well.

Before the beginning of the war, Von Lettow
personally traveled around the colony to gain
knowledge of the area and inspect his forces. After
recognizing that no conventional strategy could
possibly work against an enemy invasion, he started

---

[285] Arquilla, *Insurgents, Raiders and Bandits*, 146.
[286] Gardner, *German East*, 7.

to think of other creative ways to defend the colony with available resources. He had the ability to look at the situation with an open mind and find the right answer for the challenges he faced. Von Lettow was flexible throughout the entire war, tailoring his operations and his forces' organization as the situation required. However he had to fight not only against the Allied forces, but many times against his civilian superior, Governor Schnee. Von Lettow was convinced that German East Africa could be a key contributor in the war. He trusted in the fighting quality of his forces and based his whole irregular approach on "the native African troops, whose language he spoke and whose culture he respected."[287] Von Lettow was not only a strategic thinker, but took part in the fighting as well. He led by example; sometimes he went out as a member of a small detachment to conduct raids behind enemy lines, which once almost led to his capture by British counter-patrols.

Though he was a great strategist and

---

[287] Arquilla, *Insurgents, Raiders and Bandits*, 148.

SANDOR FABIAN

fighter, he could not succeed without his
subordinate leaders, who understood his vision and
were able from the start to lead their companies, and
later, their small detachments, in whatever was
needed. His European officers, including "Otto,
Köhl, Müller, Spangenburg, von Ruckteschell,
Kemper and von Scherbening,"[288] and his favorite
subordinate, Captain Tafel, who first figured out
and trained the German forces in how to
camouflage their head-dress by using grass and
leaves,[289] had a significant role in the success of
Von Lettow's irregular approach. Their ability to
fight without direct orders from higher headquarters
and take the initiative whenever an opportunity
presented itself made it possible for Von Lettow to
be "the only German commander to have occupied
British soil in the Great War"[290] and to have
remained undefeated.

---

[288] Paice, *Tip and Run*, 388.
[289] Gardner, *German East*, 10.
[290] Paice, *Tip and Run*, 388.

D. INTERNAL FACTORS

The first significant internal factor that needs to be considered is two handicaps with which the defense forces of German East Africa started the war. Both of these disadvantages originated from the fact that the units were originally designed to fight native warfare. First, most of the Askari units were equipped with an "old 1871 pattern rifle, using smoky powder."[291] Though this was not considered a disadvantage in battles against native fighters, who used spears, it quickly became an issue against an enemy who fought with modern armaments. "The man using smokeless powder remains invisible, while the cloud of smoke betrays the enemy with rapidity and certainty."[292] The second handicap also came from the loose character of war against natives, where "careful and thorough musketry training in the modern sense had hitherto been unnecessary."[293] The same was true for

---

[291] Von Lettow-Vorbeck, *My Reminiscences of East Africa*, 8.

[292] Von Lettow-Vorbeck, *My Reminiscences of East Africa*, 8.

training with machine guns as well. At the beginning of the war, the first problem could not be solved and it stayed a problem through the entire conflict, in the absence of resupply from the fatherland. But the second one was resolved quickly through vigorous training. The importance of rifle marksmanship and the advantages of the machine gun were quickly understood among the troops and mastered by capitalizing on the Askaris' "sharp eyesight, which enabled them to observe their fire and correct their aim accordingly."[294] These developments proved their importance from the first days of the conflict.

The next important internal factor in the success of Von Lettow's forces was the tactics used. During the initial phase of the war, German irregular tactics in the countryside were based on one unit's holding action while other nearby companies maneuvered around the enemy

---

[293] Von Lettow-Vorbeck, *My Reminiscences of East Africa*, 9.

[294] Von Lettow-Vorbeck, *My Reminiscences of East Africa*, 9.

formation in order to flank them. While Von Lettow's forces fought these battles, they continuously learned from their experiences and tried to incorporate their lessons learned into their tactics and to figure out better task organization for the fight. The battle at Tanga provides an example of this: the German companies were further broken into small combat teams built around individual machine gun and sniper nests that fired for a while, then moved to new locations.[295] The skillful positioning of these machine-gun crews and fire teams at key points, and their maneuvering capabilities, were the foundation of success, not only during the initial engagements, but until the end of the war.

Although these company-level operations were successful, when Von Lettow changed his strategy in 1915, it brought significant changes in German tactics as well. The introduction of small detachments raiding behind enemy lines led to classic guerrilla tactics. These operations initially

---

[295] Arquilla, *Insurgents, Raiders and Bandits*, 148.

were very difficult, since the war in Africa was fought without reliable maps, but as Von Lettow's forces became more trained and experienced, their operations were more and more successful.[296] The German raiders' main goal was to inflict as much damage as they could and to seize the enemy's supplies. Von Lettow's units delivered serious blows to the Uganda and Magad railways and engaged in lightning attacks against British troop columns, small outposts, supply depots, and communication sites. The small detachments "destroyed bridges, surprised guards posted on the railways, mined the permanent way and carried out raids of all kinds on the land communications between the railways and the enemy's camps."[297] Von Lettow's irregulars many times conducted ambushes as well, by using classic hit-and-run tactics. "From their ambush they opened fire on the enemy at thirty yards' range, captured prisoners and

---

[296] Gardner, *German East*, 12.

[297] Von Lettow-Vorbeck, *My Reminiscences of East Africa*, 65.

booty, and then disappeared again in the boundless desert."[298] These units understood the importance of the ability to withdraw quickly to avoid the enemy's counter-patrols. For the wounded or for those who became ill, this meant that they could not be carried with the unit. "Even the blacks understood that, and cases did occur in which a wounded Askari, well knowing that he was lost without hope, and a prey to the numerous lions, did not complain when he had to be left in the bush, but of his own accord gave his comrades his rifle and ammunition, so that they at least might be saved."[299] To further improve their destructive abilities and intelligence-gathering capabilities, the Germans established "a system of fighting patrols."[300] These units usually had twenty to thirty Askaris and one or two machine guns and were sent out to look for the enemy and provoke an engagement, like a modern

---

[298] Von Lettow-Vorbeck, *My Reminiscences of East Africa*, 64.

[299] Von Lettow-Vorbeck, *My Reminiscences of East Africa*, 66.

[300] Von Lettow-Vorbeck, *My Reminiscences of East Africa*, 66.

"movement to contact mission." As Von Lettow explained concerning the importance of these operations, "the self-reliance and enterprise of both Europeans and natives was so great that it would be difficult to find a force imbued with a better spirit."[301]

The last key internal factor was the role of intelligence. Since from almost the first day of the war, German East Africa's communications were completely cut off from the fatherland, the defense forces did not have any incoming intelligence provided by their higher command. Von Lettow barely had any idea what was going on in the European theater and he was aware that he could not expect any support from his superiors in intelligence gathering. He and his commanders had a hard time conducting proper intelligence preparation of the battlefield for their operations, since at the beginning they did not have sufficient knowledge of the area and there were no reliable maps available.[302] The main issues were with some

---

[301] Von Lettow-Vorbeck, *My Reminiscences of East Africa*, 66.

[302] Gardner, *German East*, 12.

places having multiple names and the unreliability of depicted distances, since what was "five miles on a map could mean anything from two to twenty-five miles."[303] These created confusion among the German officers, but British maps were even less reliable. Based on these facts, both sides could use only the information they collected from locals or gathered during their own operations.

The use of natives was sometimes even more confusing than the maps. Many times, the supposedly loyal natives provided incorrect directions and led their masters into an ambush by the other side.[304] Even in those cases when the natives wanted to help, their language differences and the problem with places having alternative names, led to great confusion. Von Lettow and his commanders preferred to gather intelligence first hand. During the war, the use of scouts and reconnaissance patrols was the primary means of information gathering, instead of reliance on the

---

[303] Gardner, *German East*, 12.

[304] Von Lettow-Vorbeck, *My Reminiscences of East Africa*, 66.

local population. The German units' knowledge of the terrain improved with every mission, and with this, Von Lettow's situational awareness increased as well, which many times allowed him to defeat his opponents.

E. EXTERNAL FACTORS

German East Africa was "mostly covered by dense bush, with no roads and only two railways, and either sweltering under a tropical sun or swept by torrential rain which makes the friable soil impassable to wheeled traffic; a country with occasional wide and swampy areas intercepted with arid areas where water is often more precious than gold."[305] These physical features favored Von Lettow's irregular strategy over the European-style frontal assaults preferred by the British. The German forces used the dense bushes and the limited avenues of approach, as natural obstacles restricted and channelized the movement of their

---

[305] Harry Lionel Prichard, *History of the Royal Corps of Engineers, Vol. VII*, (Chatham: The Institute of Royal Engineers, 1952), 107.

opponents, which many times drew them directly into the deadly fire of the German machine-gun teams and artillery.[306] At the same time, Von Lettow's forces used the terrain to hide their own maneuvers and get as close to their targets as possible and then melt back to the countryside. "In the thick bush, the combatants came upon each other at such close quarters and so unexpectedly, that our Askari sometimes literally jumped over their prone adversaries and so got behind them again."[307]

Beyond the challenges of the terrain, the weather of the colony also had significant effects on the operations of both sides. Malaria, the worst illness in the region, caused tens of thousands of deaths among the soldiers and carriers, and the heat, in combination with the limited water resupply, also killed many. As Von Lettow explained, "fatigue and thirst in the burning sun were so great that several men died of thirst, and even Europeans drank

---

[306] Gardner, *German East*, 80.

[307] Von Lettow-Vorbeck, *My Reminiscences of East Africa*, 66.

urine."[308] While these harsh conditions affected both sides, they were more to the favor of Von Lettow's irregulars than the Allied conventional units. One reason was that the Askaris and the German officers who had already lived in Africa before the war began were much more resistant to local illnesses and the effects of the climate than the freshly introduced Royal troops who were coming from different parts of the British Empire.[309] It was also easier for Von Lettow's units to conduct operations under these conditions, since they demanded much less logistical support than the large formations of the Allied forces. While the British needed a huge amount of food, water, and additional supplies, for the German units "a bit of game or a small quantity of booty afforded a considerable reserve of rations."[310] Von Lettow's

---

[308] Von Lettow-Vorbeck, *My Reminiscences of East Africa*, 66.

[309] The Boers are exception since they came from South Africa and for them it was easier to get used to the challenges of the climate of German East Africa.

[310] Von Lettow-Vorbeck, *My Reminiscences of East Africa*, 66.

units could resupply themselves from the field, but the British forces were too large to do so. The overall financial cost of waging the war against Von Lettow is estimated around 70 million pounds, but some comments count the overall Allied expenses at around 300 million pounds.[311] Besides the huge investment, by the final days of the conflict Von Lettow surrendered to a starving enemy and he was the one who provided food and medicine to the victors.[312]

Beyond the physical features of the colony and its climate, the population of German East Africa had a key role in the conflict as well. As mentioned, the civilian role in intelligence gathering was limited; but they still contributed significantly to the success of the Germans' irregular strategy by operating an effective economy in German-held areas. With directions from the military leadership, the population established an effective support system for the military. "Old books giving

---

[311] Paice, *Tip and Run*, 3.

[312] Arquilla, *Insurgents, Raiders and Bandits*, 154.

information about forgotten techniques of hand spinning and weaving were hunted up. Soon spinning wheels and looms were constructed; women at home and in private workshops were spinning by hand."[313] Farmers produced motor fuel from coconut, made sausages, and smoked meat, and jam and fruit juice were also produced. "Boots were made from the skins of cattle and game."[314] As a medicine, the so-called "Lettow schnapps" was made from wood bark and "those who were dosed with this draft swore its effects were worse than malaria itself."[315] Civilians with special skills were engaged in special projects. "Skilled artificers and armourers were constantly engaged with the factory engineers in the manufacture of suitable apparatus for blowing up the railways."[316] These engineers also managed to recover the SMS *Königsberg's*[317] main guns after

---

[313] Gardner, *German East*, 58.

[314] Gardner, *German East*, 58.

[315] Gardner, *German East*, 58.

[316] Von Lettow-Vorbeck, *My Reminiscences of East Africa*, 67.

she was scuttled and turned them into effective field-artillery pieces. These contributions were vital, since Von Lettow's forces were cut off from outside resupply from the beginning of the war. Sometimes a single ship, like one that reached the colony's shore in April 1915 and was run aground to avoid capture,[318] broke through the British blockade, but these rare cases did not have real effects on the final outcome of the conflict. Von Lettow and his forces fought their war in German East Africa over four years with little outside support and even mostly without any communication with the outside world against an enemy with inexhaustible resupplies.

F. CHAPTER SUMMARY AND CONCLUSION

The initial hope that the war was not going to

---

[317] SMS *Königsberg* was the only major German warship in the area at the beginning of the First World War. Initially she managed to escape from the Royal Navy and conducted several surprise raids along the coast of German East Africa. Finally she was trapped in the Rufiji river delta and sunk by the two British river monitors, the *Severn* and the *Mersey* on 11 July 1915.

Paice, *Tip and Run*, 114-122.

[318] Von Lettow-Vorbeck, *My Reminiscences of East Africa*, 67.

be taken to Africa quickly disappeared, since the strategic interest of the European countries called for action in their colonies as well. German East Africa started the First World War as a colony of Germany. Its communication and supply lines were quickly cut off from the fatherland and the colony was forced to fight independently as a small state against an inexhaustible enemy. At the beginning of the conflict, German East Africa had its own defense forces in place, consisting of conventionally organized and trained units. However the colony's size and location made it impossible to defend by conventional defensive strategy. Knowing this, the British expected a short campaign and a quick victory against the German colony, but they underestimated several key factors that made it possible for the war in German East Africa to last four years and cost the British Empire "more money and three times as many lives, if deaths from disease involving porters as well as combatants are included, than did the whole South African War [The Boer War]."[319]

From the outset, the commander of the German forces, Paul Emil Von Lettow-Vorbeck, did not even try to wage a conventional war. Instead he quickly introduced an irregular approach with which the British could not deal for a long time. It seemed a risky step, but since he built his irregular force around an already existing, professional military organization, it provided much more advantage than disadvantage. Von Lettow could fight an irregular war because he had been exposed to such an operational environment and this knowledge proved vital to his success. His company-level swarming strategy not only prevented the naval and land invasion of German East Africa, but allowed him to take the initiative. The switch to small-unit offensive operations achieved a remarkable result, since it forced the British to turn to a defensive strategy and to hold on to their own territory. This approach also forced the British to introduce and sustain a large force in Africa, which was one of Von Lettow's major

---

[319] Gardner, *German East*, 194.

strategic goals. His irregular approach provided a framework for the German defenders in which they could switch between strategic defense and offense as needed, frustrating the enemy. Many times, when the British believed that their victory was imminent, the war took a new and troubling turn.

Second, irregular tactics were better suited to the physical environment of German East Africa than the European style of warfare. The rough terrain and weather provided operational advantages for the small, swift-moving German units, while it caused serious difficulties for the Allied troops, who maneuvered in large masses. The thick bushes, the dry and hot desert, and the swamps were force multipliers for Von Lettow's forces, used as natural obstacles to block the enemy's movement and as cover and concealment to hide the irregulars' maneuvers. Climate and disease also favored the local irregulars and had a serious negative effect on the combat readiness of the arriving British troops, killing tens of thousands of them.

The third critical factor in the success of the

irregulars was their ability to switch among unit organizations and tactics, based on the requirements of the strategic environment. The German forces deployed company-size elements in positional defense with the objective to hold, while other swarming elements were ready to outflank the enemy. When the situation changed, these same units were broken down into eight-to-ten-man elements and delivered striking blows against the enemy, gaining intelligence and resupplies. After the introduction of fresh British imperial troops, the German military units were once again reorganized and went back to company-size operations. While Von Lettow's forces went through this process, they continuously learned from their previous operations and adopted these lessons into their next moves. This process and the transformation of the German units were made possible by decentralized leadership and exceptional small-unit leaders who could fight based on simple understanding of Von Lettow's strategic intent, but without direct orders.

Last but not least, the Germans' ability to

resupply themselves without relying on outside support was a key factor in the success of the irregular approach. The British enjoyed open resupply lines through the sea, but they had to feed and dress a large army. The Germans had the advantage of needing to resupply only a small force. "The total numbers enrolled in the Force during the war were about 3,000 Europeans and 11,000 Askaris. These figures include all non-combatants, such as those employed on police duty, medical personnel, supply and maintenance services, etc."[320] Von Lettow's forces could sustain themselves from the field, captured booty, and effective management of the economy in German-held areas. An indicator of the efficiency of the German resupply system was that, when Von Lettow's forces reentered German East Africa in the fall of 1918 from Mozambique, they were almost "returning to near complete fitness;"[321] and when they later surrendered, they shared their rations with the

---

[320] Von Lettow-Vorbeck, *My Reminiscences of East Africa*, 19.

[321] Gardner, *German East*, 187.

starving Allied units that pursued them. After seeing this, Von Lettow was curious "how many milliards it cost to try and crush our diminutive force the English themselves will presumably someday tell us. We, on the other hand, could probably have continued the war for years to come."[322]

The war in German East Africa provides some valuable insights for the theory advanced in this thesis. The German defense forces were originally organized and trained to fight traditional war, but it was clear from the start that no conventional defensive strategy could have succeeded. In other words, if they had chosen to fight a conventional war, the chances of success would have been close to zero. Second, this case highlights the importance of prior knowledge and experience in irregular warfare if one choses to fight such a war. Based on his previous exposure to irregular operational environments, Von Lettow designed a strategy that not only offered a higher chance of success, but, in fact, left the German forces undefeated. Third, the

[322] Von Lettow-Vorbeck, *My Reminiscences of East Africa*, 20.

organizational framework for the irregular strategy was the preexisting defense forces, which enabled the colonial forces to skip the painful phase of force buildup. Von Lettow simply made his units abandon conventional tactics and start engaging in irregular war. The existing structure made it possible to switch swiftly among task organizations. The cohesive units, existing small-unit procedures, and depth of military skills in general made his forces much more effective than an ad hoc, population-based insurgency would have been. Although the German units did recruit new members during the war, their integration was much easier because of the existing system. Though Von Lettow and his political counterpart, Governor Schnee, had serious differences about the way the war should proceed, the German commander managed to keep the overall strategy in his own hands and integrate every effort of the colony in support of his irregular approach. Although Germany lost World War I, it is safe to conclude that this far-off struggle between the "direct" and the "indirect" strategies in German

East Africa could well have ended with the victory of the "small state" once again.

CHAPTER 6

THE YUGOSLAV PARTISANS

A. BACKGROUND

On 1 September 1939, Nazi Germany invaded Poland and the Second World War began. Following a quick victory over its eastern neighbor, Germany started to look at its western borders. On 10 May 1940, German forces attacked Belgium, the Netherlands, Luxemburg, and France. The first three small states were overrun within a few days, while France held out a little more than a month. The unstoppable advance of German armored units, the evacuation of the British expeditionary forces at Dunkirk, and an Italian invasion on 10 June 1940 forced France to surrender on 22 June 1940. The victory over France and the British inability to counter the Germans on the Continent allowed the Nazis to conquer much of Europe during the following year.[323]

On 6 April 1941, as a "response" to a coup

---

[323] Arquilla, *Insurgents, Raiders and Bandits,* 202.

in Belgrade earlier that year, German forces, supported by some Italian, Bulgarian, and Hungarian units, invaded Yugoslavia. The country held strategic importance for Nazi Germany since it provided the "geographical link with Greece and Bulgaria, ultimately with the resources of the Middle East and North Africa."[324] The Axis powers defeated the Royal Yugoslav Army in eleven days and received its unconditional surrender on 17 April 1941. The country was quickly partitioned among its occupiers and puppet governments were introduced in many former Yugoslav areas. The quick defeat of their defense forces, the loss of national pride, and atrocities against civilians by the foreign invaders "stunned many Yugoslavians."[325] Resistance movements started to organize all over the country, but most actively "in Bosnia, Montenegro, and parts of Serbia."[326] Unfortunately these movements

---

[324] Joes, *Guerrilla Warfare,* 61.

[325] Joes, *Guerrilla Warfare,* 61.

[326] Laqueur, *Guerrilla Warfare,* 205.

initially were not only fighting against the occupiers, but against each other as well.

One of the resistance forces was "the Pan-Serb, monarchical group of a former Colonel, called Draja Mihailovitch."[327] He and his followers, who were mainly officers of the defeated Yugoslav army, were called "Chetniks" based on a former Serb nationalist movement, which fought against the Turks during previous wars. This group, backed by the Royal Yugoslav government in exile with the initial support of Churchill's cabinet, "gained momentum during the early summer of 1941,"[328] but showed no real willingness to decisively engage the occupying forces. "Cut off from help, and sometimes even from contact with the outside world, aware that the war would be long, and convinced that the Germans would lose,

---

[327] German Antiguerrilla Operations in the Balkans. 1941-1944, (Washington D.C.: Department of the Army, 1954) 20, accessed January 09, 2012, http://cgsc.cdmhost.com/cdm/singleitem/collection/p4013coll 8/id/2459.

[328] German Antiguerrilla Operations in the Balkans. 1941-1944, 20.

Mihailovich sought to conserve his forces and the lives of his countrymen for a better day."[329] According to the Chetnik point of view, it was better "to wait for the Germans to be weakened and to save one's forces until that moment arrived and a fatal stroke could be delivered."[330] Mihailovich also thought that after the end of the war, the other resistance group, the communist "partisans," would try to take power by force. To prevent this from happening became his and his organization's primary goal.[331]

The communist partisans led by Josip Broz, commonly known as Tito, also wanted to "isolate and destroy their rivals."[332] But their main goal was to liberate Yugoslavia from the invading forces. Although during a short period after the surrender of the country, the Yugoslav communists did not

---

[329] Joes, *Guerrilla Warfare,* 61-62.

[330] Gérard Chaliand, *Guerrilla Strategies. A Historical Anthology from the Long March to Afghanistan*, (Berkeley: University of California Press, 1982), 69.

[331] Joes, *Guerrilla Warfare,* 62.

[332] Laqueur, *Guerrilla Warfare,* 205.

conduct any attacks on the occupying forces, their strategy dramatically changed with Operation Barbarossa, the German offensive against Soviet Union on 22 June 1941. Following the news of the invasion of the Soviet Union, the politburo of the Yugoslav Central Committee met and made the decision that "the time for the uprising had come."[333] Tito himself wrote a "proclamation to the peoples of Yugoslavia to rise in revolt against the German, Italian, Hungarian, and Bulgarian invaders." During the same night, the secretly printed proclamation was distributed through couriers to all parts of the country and the Yugoslav partisan war began.

The initial revolt, which was mainly characterized by low-level sabotage actions and burning propaganda newspapers,[334] was easily suppressed by German forces and their Yugoslav collaborators, but the setback was not serious enough to constitute a lethal blow against the partisans. On 16 September 1941, Tito left Belgrade

---

[333] Chaliand, *Guerrilla Strategies,* 63.

[334] Chaliand, *Guerrilla Strategies,* 63-67.

and "went to the mountains to assume leadership of a more intensive struggle."[335] Tito's roughly fifteen thousand fighters conducted so many harassing operations against the occupying forces, including attacks on railways, logistics convoys, isolated garrisons, etc., that the Germans finally found them serious enough to launch a major offensive against the partisans. In November 1941, three German divisions were deployed to clear Serbia. As a result of these counterinsurgent operations, the partisans were forced to withdraw to Bosnia-Herzegovina.[336] Though they escaped, they could not rest for long, because another offensive, launched by Italians and their Croatian collaborators, drove them further south to Montenegro.[337] In this seemingly hopeless situation, Tito introduced a new idea to turn the war around. He ordered the majority of his forces to move north and "mounted a wide-ranging offensive

---

[335] Laqueur, *Guerrilla Warfare*, 216.

[336] Laqueur, *Guerrilla Warfare*, 216.

[337] Arquilla, *Insurgents, Raiders and Bandits*, 206.

with small combat formations."[338] Since the northward maneuvering units were also recruiting, the occupiers soon faced an even more distributed and more effective insurgency then before.

The Germans reacted by increasing their forces in Yugoslavia to over one hundred thousand[339] and launched numerous "encirclement operations and annihilation campaigns"[340] against Tito's forces. During these operations, thousands of partisans died and even Tito suffered injuries. But the Germans "could only deal with parts of the insurgency at any one time."[341] When they left an area, the resistance grew back immediately, sometimes stronger than before. This situation further worsened for the Germans with the surrender of the Italian forces in 1943, from whom the partisans acquired a large amount of weapons and supplies. At the end of 1943, the German High Command started to take the Yugoslav case even

---

[338] Arquilla, *Insurgents, Raiders and Bandits,* 207.

[339] Arquilla, *Insurgents, Raiders and Bandits,* 207.

[340] Joes, *Guerrilla Warfare,* 62.

[341] Arquilla, *Insurgents, Raiders and Bandits,* 207.

more seriously, because they evaluated the presence of Tito's forces' as creating a possible gateway for an Allied landing in the Balkans.[342] As a result of this threat, two additional operations were launched against the partisans, but they once again managed to escape destruction. In May 1944, the Germans, using only battalion-size elite units, conducted their last offensive against the insurgents. "Operation Rösselsprung" (Knight's Move) was a serious blow and almost ended with the capture of Tito. About six-thousand partisans were killed in this operation, but it did not achieve its goals, since "by that time the Allies were in a position to provide more effective air support"[343] to Tito's forces and the Germans were forced to withdraw.

After the failure of the last German offensive, the partisans, through the support of the British, who had earlier "abandoned the Chetniks and switched their supply and intelligence efforts"[344]

---

[342] Laqueur, *Guerrilla Warfare,* 217.

[343] Laqueur, *Guerrilla Warfare,* 217.

[344] Joes, *Guerrilla Warfare,* 62.

to Tito, started to push Germans to the North. In October 1944, the partisans and some Russian armored units liberated Belgrade and in April 1945, the last German soldier left Yugoslavia.[345]

B. IRREGULAR STRATEGY

With the quick defeat of their conventional defense forces, without possible help from the Allied powers, and with the limited actions of the impotent and self-seeking Chetniks, the only hope for the Yugoslavs against the Axis occupiers were Tito and his partisans. As Walter Laqueur explains in his book, *Guerrilla Warfare: A Historical and Critical Study*, "to the Russians, the creation of partisan units was an auxiliary weapon of the regular army to carry out certain tasks behind enemy lines; to the Yugoslavs the partisans were the army."[346] Since this communist-based resistance movement initially lacked proper organization, training, armored vehicles, and sufficient weapons

---

[345] Joes, *Guerrilla Warfare,* 62.

[346] Frederick William Deakin, *The Embattled Mountain,* (London: Oxford University Press, 1971), 100.

systems to wage a conventional war, the only strategy that seemed feasible for them was to conduct irregular war against the invaders.

At the beginning of the partisan struggle, the Axis forces were successful, forcing the partisans to withdraw to the south as far as Montenegro's impassable mountains where "the rough terrain made it hard for the enemy forces to get at them, but it was even harder for the insurgents to strike back from the remote mountain fastnesses."[347] Although before this event the partisans conducted numerous guerrilla-type, low-level operations, this crisis was the point when Tito formed the partisans' irregular strategy. "Tito had realized that the strength of the partisan movement lay in its dispersal, that the establishment of one compact front would be more than dangerous."[348] His new approach combined numerous already deployed tactics and procedures, including guerrilla tactics, unit reorganization, high levels of mobility, and dispersion, with the concept

---

[347] Arquilla, *Insurgents, Raiders and Bandits,* 206.
[348] Laqueur, *Guerrilla Warfare,* 217.

of, as John Arquilla names it in his book, *Insurgents, Raiders and Bandits: How Masters of Irregular Warfare Have Shaped Our World*, "the strategic swarm."

As the foundation of this new approach, Tito directed his commanders to divide and disperse their forces and attack to the north. Tito's companion Vladimir Dedijer explains the brilliance in this move when he notes:

> The enemy did not expect our offensive. Tito selected his line of advance in a masterful fashion, the demarcation line of the occupation zone of the Italian and German army. While the enemy generals were making up their minds who should attack and where, and who would stop the advance of the brigades, town after town fell, garrisons surrendered, and hundreds of new fighting men joined the proletarian brigades.[349]

During their maneuvers, the partisan units conducted effective recruitment among the population, which dramatically increased the number of insurgents. Although there were plenty

---

[349] Chaliand, *Guerrilla Strategies*, 79.

of people who wanted to fight the invaders, the partisans sometimes "deliberately drew down German punishments on the populace in order to obtain more recruits."[350] When the swarming units appeared all over Yugoslavia, the Axis forces faced the fact that instead of successfully cleaning out the partisans, the insurgency was erupting in numerous places at the same time. The wide dispersion of partisan forces and their continuously increasing number made it impossible for the occupiers to deal with them decisively. "When counterinsurgent forces moved to deal with a threat emanating from another area, the seemingly hacked-off limb of the resistance in the province they had just come from grew back, often stronger than before."[351] As a support of this strategy to maintain their local advantages and to weaken the Axis ability to counter them, the partisans systematically hunted down and killed Yugoslav collaborators, especially police officers.[352] With these actions, they not only

---

[350] Joes, *Guerrilla Warfare,* 62.

[351] Arquilla, *Insurgents, Raiders and Bandits,* 206.

sent a strong message to the general public and possible future collaborators, but also took away the Axis powers' "insider" support. This was significant, since the Axis forces tried numerous things to counter Tito's brilliant approach. They conducted not only conventional offensive operations against the partisans, but introduced numerous tested methods, including General Kitchener's idea of combining blockhouses and sweeping units from the Boer War and the use of "pseudo-gangs."[353] "The overall effectiveness of these units was enhanced by their employment of local collaborators who could speak correct dialect and help carry off the deception that these hunter–killers were just fellow fighters from another nearby units."[354] Although these methods showed some success, there was one more part of Tito's strategy that effectively countered them: the partisans' ability to share their information and increasing

---

[352] Chaliand, *Guerrilla Strategies,* 66-67.

[353] Arquilla, *Insurgents, Raiders and Bandits,* 208.

[354] Arquilla, *Insurgents, Raiders and Bandits,* 209.

knowledge of "how to outfox the hunters."[355] Tito's irregular approach was the main reason that "Yugoslavia is one of the few cases in history in which a partisan movement liberated a country and seized power largely without outside help."[356]

C. ORGANIZATION AND LEADERSHIP

The Yugoslav Communist Party, as an illegal organization before the war, had extensive knowledge in organizing and operating underground. Tito himself built and led a network of secret cells before the war, which "would prove highly useful during the years of resistance to the Nazis."[357] In addition to this, many of these cell members had operational experience, since several hundred of them fought in the Spanish Civil War.[358] Initially these cells and the communist party members formed the core of the resistance and the

---

[355] Arquilla, *Insurgents, Raiders and Bandits*, 208.

[356] Laqueur, *Guerrilla Warfare*, 219.

[357] Arquilla, *Insurgents, Raiders and Bandits*, 205.

[358] Laqueur, *Guerrilla Warfare*, 215.

partisan movement was built around them. On 27 June 1941, in order to form the strategy for the armed struggle and to direct the partisan forces, the politburo of the Yugoslav Central Committee established the general headquarters of the National Liberation Partisan Detachments, or G.H.Q. This organization "included all the members of the Politburo of the Central Committee and was subsequently expanded to include certain military leaders."[359] In September 1941, partisan commanders from all territories of Yugoslavia met in a small village called Stolica and decided to establish a G.H.Q. in every province of Yugoslavia to facilitate effective coordination among different partisan units. [360] The already existing G.H.Q. became the supreme headquarters, led by Tito. This organization provided the essential unity of leadership for the partisan movement to be successful. In November 1942, the supreme headquarters was also replaced by an even more

---

[359] Chaliand, *Guerrilla Strategies,* 64.
[360] Chaliand, *Guerrilla Strategies,* 70.

integrated command and control element when the
Anti-Fascist Council of Yugoslavia was established.

When Tito took operational command, the
partisan movement numbered about fifteen-
thousand fighters.[361] The partisan units "were
organized on a regional basis, taking as a unit
designation the name of their leader or of the area,
or of such geographical features as forests or
mountains."[362] Initially the basic units were the so-
called "odreds" or groups, which later became
partisan brigades. Some of these units stayed locally
deployed throughout the entire war, but some
brigades were also organized as mobile units,
deployed wherever they were needed to reinforce
local groups. As the war continued and the partisans
become stronger and their numbers increased, more
conventional military designations, including
division and corps, appeared as well. However these
designations most of the time were not real
indications of the strength of these units. They were

[361] Arquilla, *Insurgents, Raiders and Bandits,* 205.
[362] German Antiguerrilla Operations in the Balkans.
1941-1944, 31.

frequently used to deceive the Axis forces about the actual size of the partisan units they were facing. Many times the organization of the insurgent units greatly differed, based on their casualties or the effectiveness of their recruitment. In general, the number of partisan fighters in a brigade seldom exceeded a few hundred.[363] By the fall of 1942, the number of partisan fighters "increased to over 150,000 fighting men, divided into two corps with nine divisions, 36 brigades, and 70 separate battalions in 70 detachments."[364]

Although the establishment of high-level headquarters and conventional unit designations suggest centralized command and control, the opposite was true for the partisan movement. To be able to effectively control this irregular force and achieve success, the partisan movement needed exceptional leaders with the ability to act on their own initiative based on broad strategic frameworks. As was mentioned earlier, the main figure behind

---

[363] German Antiguerrilla Operations in the Balkans. 1941-1944, 31.

[364] Chaliand, *Guerrilla Strategies,* 81.

the partisan strategy was Tito: a man who was, as Walter Laqueur explains, "a great political and military leader, imperturbable, a man of iron will, a true believer yet not a fanatic." Tito also had significant conventional military experience from serving in the Austro–Hungarian Army during the First World War. "He distinguished himself in battle and was soon promoted to sergeant major, the youngest in the Austro–Hungarian Army."[365] In 1915, Tito was wounded and became a prisoner of war in Russia. He gained more operational experience following his release; during the Bolshevik revolution, he fought in the Russian Civil War on the Red side. Tito returned to Yugoslavia in 1920 and started to build an underground network of communist cells all over the country.[366] Before the Second World War, Tito proved that as a political leader, he was a great organizer and had the ability to influence people. He continued to act along this line during the war, since he effectively

---

[365] Arquilla, *Insurgents, Raiders and Bandits,* 204.

[366] Arquilla, *Insurgents, Raiders and Bandits,* 204-205.

suppressed the Chetniks while further expanding the communist party's influence. His biggest political achievement was to unify the various Yugoslav minorities to fight against a common enemy. As a military leader, he also possessed some crucial abilities. He was not caught in a "cognition trap" formed by his previous experiences in fighting a conventional war. Tito could also learn from the serious reverses he had many times suffered. He was able to form a "new concept of operations that would ultimately defeat smart, tough, and more numerous foes."[367] His achievements were even admired by his enemies. Heinrich Himmler said about him in 1944, when Tito was appointed marshal of Yugoslavia, that "I wish we had in Germany a few dozen Titos, a man with such a strong heart and such good nerves; he has really earned the title of marshal."[368]

---

[367] Arquilla, *Insurgents, Raiders and Bandits,* 205.

[368] Bradley F. Smith and Agnes Peterson, *Heinrich Himmler Geheimreden 1933 bis 1945*, (Propyläen Verlag, 1974), 242.

Whatever Tito's role in the successful struggle of the partisans, he could not have achieved all this success without the support of his subordinate leaders. Initially, as a rule, local party officials assumed the leadership of the partisan detachments. These leaders had a wide variety of military skills, but some were very agile and able to significantly contribute to the success of the irregular strategy. Tito's best commanders included "a Kardelj, and a Djilas, a Ribar and a Popovic, willing to accept his authority, yet able to act independently."[369] They were so capable of independent action serving the overall strategic goals that all Tito had to do during a major strategic briefing was point to one of his subordinates then point to the map, and they knew what to do.[370]

D. INTERNAL FACTORS

The Yugoslav partisans used a wide range of irregular tactics during their struggle against the

---

[369] Laqueur, *Guerrilla Warfare,* 216.

[370] Arquilla, *Insurgents, Raiders and Bandits,* 204.

Nazi occupiers. Their operational methods varied from individual action to division-level maneuvers, depending on the period of the war and the resources available. At the beginning of the resistance, the small, two-to-three member, partisan detachments conducted newspaper burnings to counter German propaganda and attacked single Axis soldiers and vehicles and Yugoslav police stations, with the aim of seizing weapons and harassing the invaders. Since during the initial period of the war the biggest issue for the partisans was a weapons shortage, they conducted these operations with axes, homemade weapons, or sometimes unloaded sport rifles. For example, in Kragujevac, a partisan detachment including 600 fighters "obtained its first six army rifles by disarming a police post."[371] The Kraljevo detachment got its first submachine gun when a local peasant struck a German motorcyclist soldier with an ax while he was riding through town.[372]

---

[371] Chaliand, *Guerrilla Strategies,* 66.
[372] Chaliand, *Guerrilla Strategies,* 67.

Throughout the entire war, the enemy was the primary source for partisan resupply. They obtained weapons from individual soldiers or from entire enemy units, such as the ten Italian divisions that left the war in 1943.[373]

The issue of weapons was very significant, since the "training of the guerrillas centered about the use of rifles and light automatic weapons, the laying of mines, and the preparation of demolitions."[374] Those partisans who previously served in the military received two-week training, while those who had no previous military experience received a four-to-six-week basic training. "The intensity of training depended to a large extent on the ability of the local commander and the need for the troops in operations."[375] The partisans' training also emphasized the importance of stealth, long night marches, and the paramount

---

[373] Laqueur, *Guerrilla Warfare,* 216.

[374] German Antiguerrilla Operations in the Balkans. 1941-1944, 33.

[375] German Antiguerrilla Operations in the Balkans. 1941-1944, 33.

role of dispersion, security, and the avoidance of battle in open areas. The insurgents built their tactics around these principles. The most frequently used irregular tactics were sabotage, raid, and ambush, but when there was an opportunity, the partisans were also capable of massing large formations, for example during operations aimed at liberating towns. Most of the time, the irregular actions were deployed in combination with propaganda activities as well.

The sabotage operations "were seldom executed on the spur of the moment, or because of a chance opportunity. As a rule they were carried out according to a plan based upon long observation. The guerrillas were intent always on making sure that the risk involved was not disproportionate to the chances of success."[376] The main targets of the sabotage operations were "airfields, railway stations, public-utility installations, ammunition and

---

[376] Alexander Ratcliffe, *Partisan Warfare. A Treatise Based on Combat Experiences in the Balkans*, (Munich:Historical Division Headquarters US Army, Europe,1953), 15.

fuel depots, and motor pools."[377] The goals behind these attacks were not only to cause casualties, but to create effective distractions among the Axis forces. "Roads were mined and blocked, particularly at bends or winding curves. The mines and obstacles were placed at points which could not be bypassed."[378] The sabotage actions were "designed to cripple transportation and communications and cause casualties, these tactics also tied down engineer personnel who might have been put to other tasks or made available for assignment to active fronts."[379] These operations were often conducted in conjunction with raids.

The raids were aimed at destroying enemy units while seizing their supplies. Raids were conducted only after a long observation of the surroundings of the target and gaining detailed knowledge of its defense, avenues of approach, and escape routes. "As a rule partisans attacked at night;

[377] Ratcliffe, *Partisan Warfare,* 16.

[378] Ratcliffe, *Partisan Warfare,* 16.

[379] German Antiguerrilla Operations in the Balkans. 1941-1944, 34.

in the morning after roads and railways had been searched for mines; or during the last hours of the day, so that in case of failure darkness would make pursuit impossible and there would be no way for systematic countermeasures to be taken the same day."[380] These operations were well planned and so "timed that the attackers would be well away before the arrival of any relief: mobile units would retire to prearranged hiding places, and the militiamen would return to their homes and regular occupations."[381] If the partisans' location was discovered, they tried to avoid battle. They hid their weapons and any insignia demonstrating their involvement in insurgent activity and tried to escape by pretending to be refugees, only to regroup somewhere else to resume fighting later.[382] As in raiding, the partisans frequently used ambushes.

The targets of the ambushes mainly consisted of small enemy detachments, enemy

---

[380] Ratcliffe, *Partisan Warfare,* 19.
[381] German Antiguerrilla Operations in the Balkans. 1941-1944, 34.
[382] Ratcliffe, *Partisan Warfare,* 22.

supply convoys, and trains, including hospital and ambulance convoys as well.[383] "Ambushes, for the most part, were laid at defiles, road bends, valleys, dense forests, places where the nature of the terrain subdued the noise of battle, and places where it would be difficult for the attacked troops to deploy for action, or escape."[384] The partisans used ambushes not only for offensive purposes; many times the German reconnaissance patrols looking for partisan hideouts were drawn into a "protective" ambush designed to trap the approaching enemy.

While the tactics of the partisan detachments in themselves were very effective, it was Tito's strategic-swarm concept that integrated them into a war-winning strategy. As Vladimir Dedijer explains:

> Such detachments could, when need arose, be welded into powerful shock units for the purpose of waging a battle that they had been compelled to accept, or could disperse and strike suddenly at the enemy and at

---

[383] German Antiguerrilla Operations in the Balkans. 1941-1944, 34.

[384] Ratcliffe, *Partisan Warfare,* 19.

definite objectives, only to disappear again from the area of the attack. The essential point was to keep the manpower as intact as possible while dealing the greatest possible blows to the enemy. The enemy should be compelled to strike into a vacuum.[385]

All the above-described tactics were effectively combined with propaganda operations, which had three main goals: undermining the invaders' morale, informing the population about the existence of the resistance, and increasing the self-confidence and morale of the partisans. These operations included the burning of German newspapers, distribution of leaflets, placement of anti-German posters, etc. As an example of these efforts, only two weeks after the beginning of the occupation, the Axis forces found posters in Belgrade saying, "Germans! We give you solemn warning. Leave Yugoslavia. Death to all Fascists! Liberty to the People!"[386] This type of propaganda

---

[385] Chaliand, *Guerrilla Strategies,* 70.

[386] Howard Fast, *Tito and his People*, (Winnipeg: Contemporary Publishers, 1944), accessed January 17, 2012, http://www.trussel.com/hf/tito2.htm.

had a serious effect on the morale of the Yugoslavs. "They whispered the slogan to one another in the streets, in the stores, in the shops, in the factories. They shouted it in their homes. It gave them courage just to hear it, just to repeat it."[387]

The high morale of the partisans increased their fighting spirit. "With rare exceptions, the partisans proved to be exceedingly tenacious, completely fearless, uncomplaining fighters."[388] But it was not only high morale that increased their effectiveness. Discipline was also strictly enforced within the insurgent detachments. The partisans were "with lesser crimes punished by public admonition, loss of rank, relief from command, or prohibition from bearing arms for a specified period of time. Serious offenses, such as treason and cowardice, were punished by death, the execution being carried out by the offender's immediate superior."[389] Beyond the irregular tactics, guerrilla

---

[387] Fast, *Tito and his People.*

[388] Ratcliffe, *Partisan Warfare,* 7.

[389] German Antiguerrilla Operations in the Balkans. 1941-1944, 34.

training, high morale, and strict discipline, there was one more important internal factor to consider.

As in every irregular struggle throughout history, intelligence served as a backbone for the partisans' operations. As was mentioned earlier, the partisans seldom conducted operations without sufficient information gathering. "A well-organized observation and spying system, based on through knowledge of the locality and the people, reached throughout the country. Its contacts extended even to the staff of the occupation forces and the offices of the police and administrative agencies. There were partisan agents among all classes of the population"[390] Throughout the war, the invaders, too, had significant numbers of collaborators with knowledge of the local terrain and language. But the partisans' effective hunting–killing operations and the population's attitude towards the collaborators allowed the Nazis only temporary advantages, such as from their pseudo-gangs, which were quickly countered. Because "women or persons who were

---

[390] Ratcliffe, *Partisan Warfare,* 13.

employed by the occupation forces as drivers, interpreters, office workers, and cleaning personnel" were collecting and reporting information for the partisans, the irregulars had a significant information advantage over their Nazi adversaries.

E. EXTERNAL FACTORS

Anthony James Joes, in his book *Guerrilla Warfare: A Historical, Biographical, and Bibliographical Sourcebook*, captures the significance of these factors in one single sentence. "Yugoslavia was a close-to-ideal setting for guerrilla war, with a population inured to hardship and combat, having a tradition of resistance to invaders, living in a land of rugged mountains, wild ravines, and thick forests, and with few rail lines or good roads."[391] For effective irregular warfare, the most significant physical feature of Yugoslavia was its wild terrain, which mostly favored the partisans and their strategy over the mechanized,

---

[391] Joes, *Guerrilla Warfare*, 63.

conventional Axis forces. "The brushy mountain country, craggy peaks, and roadless forest areas offer irregular troops numerous places to hide, opportunity to shift forces unseen even from the air, and locations for ambush."[392] The partisans could exploit the terrain during their maneuvers in both their defensive and offensive operations. "Forests, ravines, and caves protected them against attack from the air and made it easy for them to assemble and shift their forces without being observed. It was easy for them to block passes and forest paths."[393] At the same time the terrain features offered the insurgents "opportunities for enfilading attacks, ambush, raids and quick disappearance."[394]

Besides knowledge and effective military exploitation of the physical terrain, another significant external factor was the social terrain surrounding the resistance movement. The partisans, and especially Tito, managed to unify the

---

[392] German Antiguerrilla Operations in the Balkans. 1941-1944, 2.

[393] Ratcliffe, *Partisan Warfare,* 12.

[394] Ratcliffe, *Partisan Warfare,* 13.

wide variety of Yugoslav minorities against a common enemy. As with their colleagues throughout the entire history of irregular struggles, the Yugoslav partisans depended on the population as well. The effects of the Yugoslav civilians' attitudes towards the occupying forces and the countrywide intelligence service enabled the insurgents to conduct their operations based on nearly real-time, reliable information coming from all classes of the population. But the civilians not only provided information, they also supported the resistance with food and shelter. Hardly accessible mountain villages often served as hideouts for partisans during severe winter weather conditions. During these periods, the villagers provided food for the fighters as well. However, villages were seldom used as safe havens, since the partisans preferred distant mountain areas, isolated valleys, and swampy areas to establish their camps, to avoid exposing their location to possible collaborators in the villages.[395] Sometimes, they had no other

---

[395] Ratcliffe, *Partisan Warfare,* 9-10.

choice, to avoid total destruction, other than to withdraw to these near-impassable mountains. An example of this was the Axis offensive against the partisans in the fall of 1941, when they were pushed back as far as the mountains of Montenegro. Even though remote areas served the irregular strategy best, the partisans also used liberated towns as temporary strongholds, including Livno, Imotski, and Uzice, which was a location for the supreme headquarters for two months in 1941.[396] There was one more location worth mentioning in this case: the island of Bari, where Tito briefly escaped after an almost-successful German airborne raid on his camp in May 1944.[397]

As a final external factor, one must also take a look at the role of outside support in this irregular struggle. Generally speaking, one of the most remarkable things about the achievements of the Yugoslav partisans was that they succeeded with very limited outside support against a superior

---

[396] Chaliand, *Guerrilla Strategies,* 71.
[397] Arquilla, *Insurgents, Raiders and Bandits,* 210.

enemy. Their supposedly most important supporters, namely, their Russian communist comrades, initially were not able and later were not interested in helping the insurgents. The Russians "provided advice of doubtful value, but nothing else."[398] When Tito asked his comrades whether he could expect any ammunition in the near future, they replied: "You unfortunately cannot expect to get either ammunition or automatic weapons from here at an early date. The principal reason is the impossibility of getting them to you."[399] Even the redirection of Russian forces toward the end of the war was not really aimed to support Tito, but, as in other Eastern-European countries, to set the conditions for Stalin's future plans. On the other hand, the British and other Western allies initially supported the Chetniks and only switched their support to the partisans when they emerged as the primary resistance force in Yugoslavia. The British only established their permanent emissaries in 1943,

---

[398] Laqueur, *Guerrilla Warfare,* 215.

[399] Chaliand, *Guerrilla Strategies,* 76.

to coordinate the necessary support activities. The Allied forces' material supply and their operational support, especially that provided by the Allied air force, eased the job of the Yugoslav forces. But outside help did not have decisive effects.

F. CHAPTER SUMMARY AND CONCLUSION

At the beginning of the Second World War, Yugoslavia had a conventionally organized, trained, and equipped military force. It never stood a chance of defending the country against a numerically and technologically superior enemy. The Nazi forces needed only eleven days to crush the entire Yugoslav Royal Army and force its unconditional surrender. Although these occupying forces easily and quickly dealt with the conventional forces of Yugoslavia, they failed to find an effective solution against Tito's irregular forces over more than three years of sustained efforts.

One could argue that after the surrender of the Royal Army, the best Axis forces were pulled out from Yugoslavia and were sent to other fronts. But those that remained were often still victorious veterans of several campaigns. It is also questionable what would have happened if Yugoslavia had been the only adversary for the Nazi war machine. Even if these statements are valid, there are still numerous facts supporting the future strategic value of the partisans' achievements and the clear success of Tito's irregular strategy. Without providing a full list, on the Nazis' side, these facts included their initial numerical, technological, and air superiority. On the partisans' side there was a lack of outside support, arms, and unified efforts. The odds were clearly against the partisans; they succeeded because of several key conditions.

First, as in the previous cases, the Yugoslav resistance movement also had a preexisting organizational framework. In this case, it was not based on a militia system or the former conventional military, but on a previously banned, underground political party with countrywide reach and significant membership. It already had an established leadership and organizational structure. Besides those who fought in the Spanish Civil War, the majority did not have military experience, but had high levels of experience in organizing and working in complete secrecy.

Another key condition was that, besides some collaborators, who occur in any occupied country, Tito and the communist party succeeded in unifying a country with many ethnic groups against a common enemy. This unity provided an enormous advantage over the occupying forces. If one agrees that the population is the backbone of an insurgency's success, it is especially true in the case of the Yugoslav resistance. The population played numerous key roles in this struggle. The intelligence system, which contained supporters from every class of Yugoslavia's population, enabled the partisans to base their operations on reliable, real-time information and evade pursuing forces. The food and shelter provided by the civilians were many times key to the survival of entire partisan units. The resistance not only received food, shelter, and recruits from the population, but, with its high morale and resistance to the continuous Nazi brutality, it motivated the partisans to keep fighting.

Next, Tito's irregular strategy and his strategic swarm masterfully exploited the physical features of Yugoslavia. The partisans, based on their foot- and horse-mobility, were capable of using the terrain as a force multiplier while the same terrain seriously decreased the effectiveness of the motorized and mechanized Axis units. In many cases, because of the effective use of the terrain by the insurgents, the equipment and tactics the Nazis used so successfully during the fight against the conventional Yugoslav army became serious impediments to fighting the irregulars.

It was also a key to the success of the irregular strategy that the partisan leaders, especially Tito, possessed some key capabilities. Although Tito held numerous briefings and determined strategic level goals, he delegated authority to his subordinates to make decisions about how to operate. The partisan commanders were capable of taking the initiative whenever it was necessary to support the overall irregular strategy. The other key capability was their open-mindedness and ability to adapt. They learned both from their successes and failures, and when the Nazis introduced new tactics, including a Boer War-type network of strong points paired with ranger-type sweeping units, or the employment of pseudo-gangs, partisan leaders were always able to adjust and counter them effectively.[400]

Last but not least, the partisans' tactics had a huge impact on their success. Thorough planning and selective targeting avoided unnecessary loss of fighters while inflicting maximum damage on the enemy. Though the partisans intended to inflict as many casualties as possible on the Nazis, they also realized the high importance of sheer disruption. Their targets were specifically chosen to create as much chaos as possible. Attacks on railway stations, public-utility installations, and fuel depots created

---

[400] Arquilla, *Insurgents, Raiders and Bandits,* 208-210.

conditions for the occupiers that required them to commit more resources to protecting these installations than has been supposed necessary. This became more and more challenging toward the end of the war, when every piece of equipment and every single German soldier were needed on many fronts.

The Yugoslav partisans' struggle highlights some additional factors with regard to the topic of this research. In this case, a country began a war with an already existing, conventionally organized, trained, and equipped army, which surrendered after eleven days. After the country's complete defeat and occupation, a previously existing (but not military) organization, already operating underground, took over the mission to fight against the invaders. This organization, without any significant outside support, in the shadow of the enemy forces' numerical and technological superiority—and based only on its existing organizational framework and leadership—managed to build up substantial irregular forces.

These forces, by capitalizing on a brilliant irregular strategy, effectively resisted the war machine that had conquered so much of Europe, North Africa, and, temporarily, a huge part of the Soviet Union. The war between the direct and indirect strategy ended with the victory of the small state.

CHAPTER 7

THE FIRST RUSSO-CHECHEN WAR

A. BACKGROUND

Russia has been trying to extend and maintain its control over Chechnya, a small, landlocked country in the Caucasus, for a couple of centuries. As a result of aggressive Russian policy, the Chechens have been struggling to keep their independence since the early 19th century. Because of the enormous differences between large and powerful Russia, and small and weak Chechnya, the conflict has been characterized as an irregular struggle from the beginning.

The first significant clash occurred in 1816, when General Alexei Ermolov's imperial forces entered the region with the objective of subduing the Chechens and establishing a permanent Russian presence in the area. However, the initial imperial operations failed, due to fierce Chechen resistance. The peace did not last long, and war resumed in 1829. This time, the conflict lasted about 30 years and ended with the defeat of the Chechen forces, led by Imam Shamil.[401] Though the eventual Russian victory was complete, the Chechens' desire for independence never waned. A "significant portion of the [Chechen] population rallied to rebel leadership as each generation brought a new burst of resistance to Russian domination."[402] Because of this mindset, the Russians had to face an almost continuous uprising against their rule and they "never felt secure about their control of the Caucasus."[403]

The next major Chechen uprising, led by Sheikh Najmuddin, took place in 1917, during the Bolshevik Revolution. The Chechens saw the chaotic events in Russia as an opportunity to gain autonomy. They were successful at the beginning, but after the Bolsheviks gained control over Russia, they soon suppressed Chechen resistance as well. The following decades brought continuous revolts

---

[401] Arquilla, *Insurgents, Raiders and Bandits,* 254.

[402] Paul Bernard Henze, *Islam in the North Caucasus* (Santa Monica: RAND Corporation, 1995), 12.

[403] Arquilla, *Insurgents, Raiders and Bandits*, 254.

against Bolshevik rule, culminating in Stalin's brutal action in 1937, during which about 14,000 Chechens were arrested and exiled or executed.[404] The devastation of the Chechens by the Russians went further towards the end of the Second World War, when Stalin ordered the deportation of approximately 400,000 Chechens to Central Asia "in retaliation for what he viewed as their treachery."[405] About 40 percent of those who were exiled died en route to their new homes, and those who survived were not allowed to return until 1956 when, a few years after Stalin's death, Khrushchev "pardoned" the Chechens.[406] Although this was a significant act from the Soviet Union, the relationship between the Russians and the Chechens did not really change. Khrushchev restored the "traditional" Russian order by force and introduced a reintegration policy that "set a time bomb ticking

---

[404] John Boyd Dunlop, *Russia Confronts Chechnya: Roots of a Separatist Conflict*, (Cambridge: Cambridge University Press, 1998), 55.

[405] Arquilla, *Insurgents, Raiders and Bandits*, 254.

[406] Dunlop, *Russia Confronts Chechnya*, 68.

in the Caucasus."[407] As John Arquilla explains in his book, *Insurgents, Raiders and Bandits: How Masters of Irregular Warfare Have Shaped Our World*: "in the last three decades of the Cold War, Chechen nationalism did not die, but rather waited for its moment, like a tree in winter waiting for spring. That spring came with the dissolution of the Soviet Union in 1991."[408]

As many times before, the Chechens, now led by a former Soviet air-force officer, General Dzhokhar Dudayev, sensed the opportunity presented by events. On 6 September 1991, they dissolved the local pro-Soviet government and started to create the conditions necessary to declare independence. During the following months, Dudayev consolidated his power and soon was elected the first president of the Independent Chechen Republic.[409] As a response to the events in Chechnya, the Russian president, Boris Yeltsin,

---

[407] Arquilla, *Insurgents, Raiders and Bandits*, 255.
[408] Arquilla, *Insurgents, Raiders and Bandits*, 255.
[409] Arquilla, *Insurgents, Raiders and Bandits*, 255.

initially sent some internal troops to restore order, but they were quickly forced to withdraw when the Chechen forces surrounded their airplanes at Khankala airbase.

Following this embarrassment, the Russians turned to covert operations in an effort to overthrow Dudayev. During the following years, the Russians' covert effort was made possible by the fierce fighting between Dudayev's supporters and numerous opposition groups. The Russians initially provided financial support and military equipment for these groups, but since they did not manage to make enough progress, the Russians went on supplying service members as well to support anti-Dudayev operations. Russian involvement became public after one of the opposition groups, the Provisional Council, failed in its attempt to seize Grozny on 29 November 1994. At this point, Yeltsin decided to launch a full-scale offensive against Chechnya.

The Russians expected a quick victory. Their strategy was formed around the quick occupation of the Chechen capital and other key urban areas. Since the minister of defense, General Pavel Grachev did not expect any serious resistance; his plan was to conclude the war within fifteen days. [410] But when Russian troops entered Chechnya on 11 December 1994, they quickly realized that their timeline had to be changed. The Russians obtained air superiority by destroying the Chechens' 266 aircraft, but when they maneuvered through the Caucasus, they met an unexpectedly strong resistance from the local population, which inflicted casualties and seriously slowed their advance.[411] They finally reached Grozny on 26 December 1994 and, following several days of indiscriminate bombing of the city, on New Year's Eve started a siege. They entered Grozny in "three armored columns in herringbone formations"[412] and soon found themselves fighting against hundreds of

[410] Olga Oliker, *Russia's Chechen Wars 1994-2000: Lessons from Urban Combat*, (Santa Monica: Rand Corporation, 2001), 9.

[411] Oliker, *Russia's Chechen Wars 1994-2000*, 9-11.

[412] Oliker, *Russia's Chechen Wars 1994-2000*, 12.

small, highly trained, and well organized enemy units who were following a swarming-based irregular strategy, formed by the Chechen military's chief of staff, a former Russian artillery officer, Aslan Maskhadov. The Chechen defenders, who were a few thousand fighters in all and vastly outnumbered by the invaders, quickly defeated the initial Russian attacks and caused a large number of casualties.[413] For example, the 131st "Maikop" Motor Rifle Brigade was completely destroyed at Grozny's central railway station.[414] After this initial success, despite the fact that the Russians poured thousands of additional troops into the fight, the Chechens were able to hold Grozny through fierce irregular, urban combat for one more month. But even when the Chechens decided to give up the city, the war was not lost. Since Russian forces never managed to completely seal off the capital, the small irregular teams could leave the city to

---

[413] Arquilla, *Insurgents, Raiders and Bandits*, 258.

[414] Carlotta Gall and Thomas de Waal, *Chechnya: Calamity in the Caucasus*, (London: New York University Press, 1998), 177-180.

continue their fight in the rough mountainous regions.

Following the seizure of Grozny, the Russian forces started to expand their control over the rural areas. They systematically advanced from village to village to defeat the resistance. To counter these operations, the Chechen irregulars conducted holding actions as long as practicable, and then moved away from the enemy while executing continuous harassing operations against Russian troop columns and logistic nodes. By May 1995, Russian forces controlled the major towns in Chechnya and the fight was taken to the mountain villages. This period was characterized by the inability of either side to decisively engage the other. Typically, the Chechens inflicted damage on Russian forces while they were maneuvering into position to surround a mountain village. The Russians shelled the village until there was no return fire from the Chechen rebels, and then moved in. The Chechens redeployed to the next village and attacked the next moving Russian columns. In this situation, the Chechens needed to do "something very dramatic in order to arrest further Russian progress on the ground in Chechnya."[415] The Chechen leaders agreed to introduce terrorism into the repertoire of their irregular means.

On 14 June 1995, a small Chechen unit, containing about 100 fighters and led by Shamil Basayev, infiltrated into Russia using Russian military uniforms and equipment. The Chechen detachment raided the town of Budennovsk with the main objective of taking as many hostages as possible and, through them, to force a Russian withdrawal from Chechnya. During the operation, the Chechen raiders captured the town's hospital and held about 1,500 hostages. The Russians launched multiple attacks to recapture the hospital and liberate the hostages, but all of them failed, and finally the Chechens managed to negotiate a free passage back to Chechnya. The success of this operation forced the Russians to start engaging in negotiations and brought a brief cease-fire between

---

[415] Arquilla, *Insurgents, Raiders and Bandits*, 259.

the sides.[416] On 30 July 1995, both parties signed an agreement to stop military operations and the Russians promised a phased withdrawal from Chechnya. Elections were planned for the end of the year.[417] However, the increasing number of violations of this agreement on both sides during the fall, including an assassination attempt on a senior Russian officer, General Anatoliy Romanov, quickly dismissed the dream of a long-lasting peace.

On 9 January 1996, the Chechens launched another raid, this time attacking the town of Kizlyar in the Republic of Dagestan. About 200 Chechens, led by Salman Radujev, primarily targeted the local airfield to destroy Russian planes and cargo. But when they arrived at the airfield, they realized that only a few airplanes and limited cargo were there.[418] The Russians responded quickly and effectively, which forced the Chechens to withdraw. Radujev

---

[416] Dimitri V. Trenin and Aleksei V. Malashenko, *Russia's Relentless Frontier: The Chechnya Factor in Post-Soviet Russia,* (Washington, DC: Carnegie Endowment for International Peace, 2008), 23–24.

[417] Arquilla, *Insurgents, Raiders and Bandits*, 260.

[418] Arquilla, *Insurgents, Raiders and Bandits*, 260-261.

led his men with a couple of busloads of hostages to the southwest toward the Chechen border, but they were trapped by the Russian forces at the village of Pervomaiskoye. Radujev's forces entrenched themselves and continued to fight the Russians for three days, finally exfiltrating shortly before the Russians completely destroyed the village.[419] The mass media covered the events in Pervomaiskoye and "reported the excessive military and civilian casualties, causing a general public condemnation of the Yeltsin government's conduct of war."[420] However, in this sensitive situation, the Russians scored a separate success by killing the Chechen president with a rocket, after triangulating his position by tracking his satellite phone. Nevertheless, the Chechens soon took over the initiative.[421]

---

[419] Robert M. Cassidy, *Russia in Afghanistan and Chechnya: Military Strategic Culture and the Paradoxes of Asymmetric Conflict,* (Carlisle Barracks, PA: U.S. Army War College Strategic Studies Institute, 2003), 46.

[420] Cassidy, *Russia in Afghanistan and Chechnya*, 46.

[421] Stasys Knezys and Romanas Sedlickas, *The War in*

The loss of their president did not weaken the Chechens' fighting spirit. Maskhadov quickly ordered a countrywide offensive against the Russians. The Chechens attacked in the rural areas and mountains and shook up the Russian invaders. The Maskhadov offensive's main objective was Grozny. Hundreds of small Chechen units infiltrated back into the capital and "after more than two weeks of fighting that turned Grozny into a smaller-scale Stalingrad,"[422] the Russians entered negotiations with Maskhadov. The negotiation, and with it the war, ended in August 1996 when both sides signed a peace agreement in Khasavyurt.

B. IRREGULAR STRATEGY

As Robert M. Cassidy observes, "nonetheless, however much Russia had fallen from superpower status and however much Russian military power was degraded, the Russian forces that invaded Chechnya still exhibited the military

---

Chechnya, (College Station: Texas A & M University, 1999), 311–313.

[422] Arquilla, *Insurgents, Raiders and Bandits*, 262.

strategic preferences of a great power."[423] The results of the initial operations, including the quick and complete destruction of the Chechen air force made it clear that no conventional defensive strategy would have provided a significant chance for success for the Chechens against the Russian military. This recognition produced a unique irregular defensive approach, designed by Aslan Maskhadov, which allowed the Chechens to fight effectively against a superior enemy.

During the initial phase of the war, including the defense of Grozny in 1995, Maskhadov formed his strategy around urban combat, waged by hundreds of small and dispersed swarming fire teams. In Grozny, the Chechens started to give a taste of their understanding of irregular warfare, by not relying solely on traditional small-scale ambushes and hit-and-run guerrilla tactics, but by attacking larger Russian elements with the aim of destroying entire formations. They introduced a "maneuverable defense" by holding on to a position

---

[423] Cassidy, *Russia in Afghanistan and Chechnya*, 37.

one day then disappearing on the next to maneuver into new positions, which made it close to impossible for the Russians to annihilate the defenders. "The lack of fixed defenses and the mobility of the small groups of fighters were in fact their strength."[424] President Dudayev explained the essence of this strategy by saying, "strike and withdraw, strike and withdraw… exhaust them until they die of fear and horror."[425] These tactics were very effective, and through them the Chechens could hold on to the capital for a month while inflicting enormous losses on their enemy. But because the Russians poured several thousand more troops into the fight and changed some of their tactics, the Chechens were forced to withdraw from Grozny to the countryside.

Heavy losses during the defense of the capital forced Maskhadov to further modify his approach to fit rural areas and small Chechen

---

[424] Gall and de Waal, *Chechnya*, 191.

[425] Robert Seely, *Russo-Chechen Conflict, 1800-2000. A Deadly Embrace*, (New York: Frank Cass Publishers, 2004), 230.

towns. He introduced "an indirect strategy of attrition in which he avoided general actions against the Russian main efforts but instead concentrated what forces he had against weak enemy outposts and piecemeal detachments."[426] During this phase of the war, the Chechen strategy was focused on two major objectives. First, they had to keep the struggle alive by preserving their forces and exhausting the Russians with raids and other harassing operations. As one of the Chechen battle groups' deputy commanders, Khamzat Aslambekov, explained, they did not have too many choices at that time: "There is no winning. We know that. If we are fighting, we are winning. If we are not, we have lost. The Russians can kill us and destroy this land. Then they will win. But we will make it very painful for them."[427] The Russians

---

[426] Cassidy, *Russia in Afghanistan and Chechnya*, 17.

[427] Gregory J. Celestan, Wounded Bear: The Ongoing Russian Military Operation in Chechnya, 1996, accessed February 29, 2012, http://fmso.leavenworth.army.mil/documents/wounded/wounded.htm#25.

played into the hands of the Chechen strategy by falling into the same trap as many counterinsurgent forces before them did, by trying to control the country throughout the extensive use of small outposts.[428] "Once dispersed, their outposts had never been numerous enough really to control the country, because partisan raids on the smaller posts had compelled them to consolidate into fewer and fewer garrisons. But the garrisons were too few and too small to check the partisans' operations throughout the countryside."[429]

The second main objective of the Chechen strategy during this time was to break the Russian leadership's will to fight and to force the withdrawal of Russian troops from Chechen territory. During the entire war, the Chechens based their information strategy on the theme of a free nation being oppressed by an aggressor, Russia.

---

[428] This concept worked well in Anbar Province in Iraq during 2007 and 2008, but only because in this case the American forces managed to gain the support of the local population and turned them against the local Al-Qaeda fighters.

[429] Cassidy, *Russia in Afghanistan and Chechnya*, 16.

They allowed journalists to be present in hot spots and provided first-hand access to information in order to influence public opinion. Chechen leadership encouraged the journalists to report about the brutality of Russian tactics and to describe the suffering of Chechen civilians.[430] "The rebels were very open to press interest, granting interviews and generally making themselves available to domestic and foreign journalists."[431] To further influence public opinion, besides waging continuous small-scale attacks on the Russian troops, the Chechens also introduced psychological operations supported by terrorism as another form of their irregular approach. Both Basayev's raid on Budennovsk and Radujev's attack on Kizlyar were designed to stop further Russian military progress in Chechnya and targeted the will of the Russian public and

---

[430] John Arquilla and Theodore Karasik, "Chechnya: A Glimpse of Future Conflict," *Studies in Conflict and Terrorism*, Volume 22, Number 3, 1 July 1999, 217, accessed March 05, 2012, http://www.ingentaconnect.com/content/routledg/uter/1999/00000022/00000003/art00003.

[431] Oliker, *Russia's Chechen Wars 1994-2000*, 22.

politicians. These actions were successful not only because most of the raiding force got back home safely after negotiations, but because the events were covered by the Russian mass media. In this regard, Basayev's raid was more successful than Radujev's operation, since as a result of the first event, a cease-fire agreement was signed, promising phased Russian troop withdrawals and elections at the end of 1995. But these never happened, and the war soon resumed with full intensity.

Following the death of President Dudayev in April 1996, Maskhadov ordered a countrywide offensive against the Russian troops, "a campaign that looked much like Vo Nguyen Giap's 1968 Tet offensive."[432] Several thousand Chechen fighters organized into small fire teams attacked the Russian forces in rural and urban areas simultaneously, all over the country. The major objective of this offensive was Grozny. The Chechen fighters, split into around a hundred small units, infiltrated the capital and for the next two weeks engaged 12,000

---

[432] Arquilla, *Insurgents, Raiders and Bandits*, 261.

Russian troops in fierce fighting. This seems to have been enough for the Russian leadership, and especially for President Yeltsin, since he sent his advisor on security affairs, Alexander Lebed, a former army general and Afghanistan veteran, to negotiate the conditions for peace with Maskhadov. Since the Russians were willing to meet the most important Chechen request, to withdraw their forces from Chechnya, an agreement was soon reached and the fighting ended.[433]

C. ORGANIZATION AND LEADERSHIP

The Chechen military forces in 1991, according to Major General Sokolov, the commander of the Russian north Caucasian military district at that time, consisted of 62,000 fighters in the national guard and an additional 30,000 in the militia.[434] By 1994, these forces were augmented with Shamil Basayev's 350 men from the Abkhazian battalion, 250 men under the command

---

[433] Arquilla, *Insurgents, Raiders and Bandits*, 261-262.
[434] Dunlop, *Russia Confronts Chechnya*, 116.

of Ruslan Galayev, an artillery detachment with 30 artillery pieces, an armored unit containing fifteen tanks, and the Chechen ministry of the interior's force, consisting of 200 fighters.[435] Despite the fact that shortly after their independence the Chechens planned to build a conventional military in order to prove the capabilities of their country, at the beginning of the war their organization was remarkably flat, taking a "network" form of organization.[436] This irregular organization was a result of two factors. First, Aslan Maskhadov recognized that an open, conventional war against Russia would end in disaster for Chechnya and he encouraged the subdivision and dispersion of the Chechen forces. The second factor was that throughout history, the organization of the Chechen forces had a direct link to the social structure of Chechnya. This structure was based on clan

[435] Ib Faurby and Marta-Lisa Magnusson, "The Battle(s) of Grozny," *Baltic Defense Review*, 2/1999, 77, accessed March 06, 2012,
http://www.bdcol.ee/files/docs/bdreview/07bdr299.pdf.

[436] Arquilla and Karasik, "Chechnya: A Glimpse of Future Conflict," 212.

formations. As Theodore Karasik explains this phenomenon:

> Chechen clans, called *taip*, identify member descent from a common ancestor twelve generations removed. A particular *taip* might consist of two to three villages of 400 to 600 people each and supply 600 fighters. For combat purposes, these groups are broken down into units of 150 and further subdivided into squads of about 20 for combat operations that work one-week shifts, one after the other.[437]

Despite serious feuds occurred among the taips, this type of social structure, with its unifying power against a common enemy, connectivity, and durability provided an ideal framework for the irregular war that the Chechens fought between 1994 and 1996 against Russia.

As Olga Oliker explains, "Russian and Chechen sources agree that nonstandard squads were the basis of the rebel force."[438] These squads

---

[437] Theodore Karasik, "Chechen Clan Tactics and Russian Warfare," CACI Analyst, 15 March 2000, accessed March 05, 2012, http://cacianalyst.org/?q=node/353

[438] Oliker, *Russia's Chechen Wars 1994-2000*, 19.

consisted of fifteen to twenty fighters subdivided into fire-team-sized cells. Each fighter within these small elements was armed with different kinds of weapon systems, including RPG-7s, RPG-18s, machine guns, and Dragunov sniper rifles, to increase unit effectiveness. Usually several fighting cells were deployed as "hunter–killer teams" against armored targets. "The sniper and machine gunner pin down Russian supporting infantry, while the antitank gunner engages the armored target. Normally, five or six hunter–killer teams attack an armored vehicle in unison and can force serious delays in Russian actions."[439] These small elements eventually could form a larger unit, consisting of 25 men, including ammunition bearers, medics, and supply personnel. If it was operationally necessary, three of these 25-man units could be further combined into a 75-man element, which was augmented with a highly mobile mortar crew. These units played a key role in urban

---

[439] Karasik, "Chechen Clan Tactics and Russian Warfare."

combat, since the Chechens usually divided the cities into quadrants and a 75-man element was responsible for the defense of an individual quadrant.[440] Besides the use of these units, the Chechens also deployed individual snipers or small sniper teams to inflict as many casualties as possible and create fear among the Russian troops. Olga Oliker noted that "Chechen snipers, whether operating alone or as part of an ambush group, nightly terrified Russian soldiers, who dubbed them ghosts."[441] The snipers were so effective that, in one instance, out of an entire Russian battalion only ten soldiers and one staff officer survived their accurate fire.[442]

These organizational elements provided unique flexibility for the rebels. Their organizational simplicity and durability allowed the widely dispersed small units to conduct self-coordinated attacks, but also gave them the ability

---

[440] Oliker, *Russia's Chechen Wars 1994-2000*, 19.

[441] Oliker, *Russia's Chechen Wars 1994-2000*, 21.

[442] Knezys and Sedlickas, *The War in Chechnya*, 106.

to reorganize into larger formations when needed. Still, the effective organizational characteristics of the Chechen forces would have not been enough for success. To capitalize on these characteristics, capable military leaders were also much needed.

At the strategic level, the Chechen leaders had to understand the traditional Chechen fighting organization and form a strategy that would capitalize on its advantages to create a chance against a numerically and technologically superior enemy. The president of Chechnya, Dzhokhar Dudayev, and the chief of staff of the Chechen military, Aslan Maskhadov were such leaders. Both of them were trained and educated in the Russian military. The president previously served in the Russian air force as a general officer, while the latter was an artillery colonel. Dudayev was more involved in the political aspects of the struggle, while Maskhadov was primarily responsible for the defensive military strategy of Chechnya.[443] Based on his prior military experience, Maskhadov

---

[443] Arquilla, *Insurgents, Raiders and Bandits*, 255.

understood the strengths and weaknesses of both sides. He could form a strategy that not only exploited Russian weaknesses, but also made the most of Chechen strengths. He tested his approach during the initial skirmishing between Dudayev's supporters and the pro-Moscow movements between 1992 and 1994. His vision of commander's-intent-based operations, which relied on highly decentralized execution and small-unit level coordination, proved to be very effective not only during this initial conflict, but throughout the entire war against the Russians. As his motto said, "less centralization, more coordination."[444] He continuously learned from engagements and developed his irregular approach. Maskhadov was capable of facing reality and fought only when it was practicable. His main goal was to keep the struggle alive while he tried to shape the battlefield through harassing raids, terrorist acts, and other irregular means to set the conditions to take over the initiative. When the time arrived, he launched an

---

[444] Knezys and Sedlickas, *The War in Chechnya*, 107.

offensive against the Russian forces, which "provides either evidence of one of history's most exceptional military miracles or a persuasive example of the inherent superiority of a small, swarming irregular force against a traditionally organized opponent. In either case, a true master of the battlefield emerged to carry it off."[445]

Maskhadov's strategy could only work if he had capable subordinate leaders with the ability to act along the lines of his irregular strategy. Since his entire strategy was based on hundreds of small elements capable of acting by themselves or as a part of slightly larger formations, the question of small-unit leadership was crucial to the success of the Chechen struggle. These leaders indeed possessed those capabilities and were the backbone of the Chechen strategy's success. They not only led their fire-team-sized units into battle, but were able to coordinate for larger-scale attacks to increase their effectiveness and maximize Russian casualties. Stasys Knezys and Romanas Sedlickas

---

[445] Arquilla, *Insurgents, Raiders and Bandits*, 259-260.

described the effectiveness of the small Chechen elements and their leaders in more detail by stating that:

> During the repulsion of the assault [in Grozny] the Chechen forces operated almost independently. Many small groups of Chechen fighters in the city also found themselves appropriate places in the city's defenses. Everyone's basic purpose was, after all, the same: to destroy the enemy. These mobile, completely independent groups chose their targets themselves and, being always on the move, created for the Russian units the appearance of a unified attack. The coordination among the leaders of the Chechen fighter groups was, however, exceptional. Even without centralized command, they succeeded in fighting their opponent all over the city simultaneously.[446]

These small units were very effective in the capital and they did not disappear after they had to give up Grozny. After fleeing the capital by multiple routes toward the mountainous areas, the Chechen leadership was able to reestablish the fighting network in a short time. The leaders continued to

---

[446] Knezys and Sedlickas, *The War in Chechnya*, 107.

learn and adapt during the entire war, which allowed them to extend their control all over those rural areas that were not physically occupied by the Russians.

D. INTERNAL FACTORS

One of the significant internal factors that led to the success of the Chechens was the high level of pre-conflict military training among their fighters. The centuries-old armed struggle against Russia, in combination with Chechnya's militant society, provided an excellent foundation for a civil-militia based, irregular force, but the Chechen fighters had much more training and experience to capitalize on. By 1991, the major part of the Chechen male population had gone through military training in Russia and of those "who were not veterans of the Soviet/Russian armed forces, a good number may have trained abroad, for instance in Azerbaijan, Pakistan, or Turkey."[447] Since the Russians trained the Chechens from the tactical to

---

[447] Oliker, *Russia's Chechen Wars 1994-2000*, 17.

the strategic level, they were not only capable of operating their weapons and conducting missions effectively, they also knew the Russians' order of battle, the capabilities of their military systems, and their tactics in different operational environments. The Russians even played into the hands of the Chechens by training, arming, and deploying the Abkhaz battalion, a Chechen-based unit deployed in the First Georgian Abkhaz War. The personnel of this unit were rotated on a regular basis, which gave thousands of Chechens training and operational experience in fierce urban combat before the Russo–Chechen War. Additionally, a large number of Chechen fighters received training in "mountain guerrilla fighting," based on the Russian experience in the Soviet–Afghan War. The Chechens were also trained in night operations, which, especially at the early stage of the war, provided a huge advantage over the Russian forces.[448]

This pre-conflict training made the Chechen

---

[448] Arqilla and Karasik, "Chechnya: A Glimpse of Future Conflict," 210.

forces very effective, but they never stopped training during the war. They continuously evaluated the lessons from engagements and made significant efforts to come up with new procedures to fight the Russians more effectively. As Arquilla and Karasik explain, "these groups 'commuted' from their homes to the field of battle. While home, they would share, through story-telling sessions, their latest experiences with other units of the taip, offering advice about how to fight the Russians, as well as technical tips about such matters altering grenade launchers with saws to provide them with more velocity."[449]

Concerning tactics used by the Chechens during the war, one can say that they utilized every imaginable and seemingly unimaginable way to fight their opponents. The tactical foundation of the Chechen irregular struggle was the swarm. By mastering this concept, the Chechens were able to effectively confront larger conventional formations.

---

[449] Arquilla and Karasik, "Chechnya: A Glimpse of Future Conflict," 210.

Small mobile teams defeated large armored formations through turning the strength of these weapon systems into weaknesses. "They learned to hit the front and rear vehicles of Russian convoys first, in order to immobilize the convoy, then struck at close range with sawed-off RPGs—shorter barrels made for greater velocity—that had napalm charges attached, starting fire inside and often blowing up the invaders' tanks."[450] As a result of these tactics, the Chechens destroyed a couple of dozen Russian tanks during the first month of the fighting in Grozny. The use of sniping and the deployment of mines and improvised, explosive devices also proved to be a very effective tactic in the rebel repertoire. They were successful not only because they caused a large number of casualties and terrified the Russian soldiers, but because the reaction to these types of attacks slowed the Russian forces down, which made them vulnerable to swarming.

Chechen tactics did not pose a threat to the

---

[450] Arquilla, *Insurgents, Raiders and Bandits*, 258.

Russian ground units only; the rebels were very successful in destroying air assets, including attack and cargo helicopters, as well. As Karasik explains:

> Chechen mobile air defense weapons are controlled by radio and change positions constantly, hampering the Russians' ability to detect and destroy them. The Chechen forces also lure Russian air assets into specially prepared "kill zones." Chechen forces jam Russian radio transmissions and use radio direction finding equipment to hunt and kill Russian controllers that guide Russian forces to targets. When Chechens knock down Russian helicopters, they swarm their small combat teams to Russian landing zones hitting them with machine gun, sniper and RPG fire.[451]

The Chechen forces also used deception and psychological warfare on many occasions. The Chechen fighters got through Russian checkpoints by wearing Russian uniforms or appearing as refugees using forged documents. Other times they "disguised themselves as Red Cross workers, donning the identifying armbands. They also passed

---

[451] Karasik, "Chechen Clan Tactics and Russian Warfare."

themselves off as civilians and offered to guide Russian forces through the city, instead leading them into ambushes."[452]

Since at the initial stage of the war the Russians mainly used open radio channels, the Chechen irregulars were also able to transmit misleading radio messages and conflicting orders, which caused great confusion among the Russian troops. The Chechens' psychological operations had two main objectives. The first was to terrify the Russian soldiers and weaken their fighting spirit. The second was to influence the Russian public and, through them, the Russian leadership. In order to reach these goals, the Chechens employed different operational measures from "hanging Russian wounded and dead upside down in the windows of defended positions, forcing the Russians to fire at their comrades in order to engage rebels"[453] to conducting terrorist attacks deep into Russia. The rebels also used mobile television and radio

---

[452] Oliker, *Russia's Chechen Wars 1994-2000*, 21.

[453] Karasik, "Chechen Clan Tactics and Russian Warfare."

platforms to communicate their messages while jamming the Russian efforts to transmit in Chechnya. The Chechens influenced public opinion by allowing a large number of international journalists to be present in Grozny and other hot spots. Sometimes the Chechens manipulated events to further support their agenda. As Oliker explains, "the few tanks the rebels had were dug into multistory buildings in the center of the city. When the Chechens fired from these positions, Russian returned fire inevitably hit civilian housing, schools, hospitals, and daycare centers. When the cameras recorded and sent these images home, the Russians looked especially heartless, and the Chechens appeared even more the victims."[454]

The last significant internal factor influencing the outcome of the First Russo–Chechen War was the information advantage possessed by the rebels. Since a large portion of the Chechens had trained in the Russian army, they knew the enemy's tactics, techniques, and procedures. The Chechens knew the

---

[454] Oliker, *Russia's Chechen Wars 1994-2000*, 22.

capabilities and the limitations of the Russian weapons systems and, through this knowledge, how to counter them. "Knowing to avoid the reactive armor at the front of the Russian tanks (which a number of the T-72s and T-80s went into battle without), the rebels focused their fire on the top, rear, and sides. They also knew how to attack vulnerable APCs such as the BMP-1."[455] Simply put, the rebels could think with the Russian mind, which gave them an enormous advantage. The use of open-channel radio communication on the Russian side also provided a significant advantage, since the Chechens could hear and, since all of them spoke Russian, understand everything the Russians said. Based on this intelligence, the rebels could easily prepare their operations, since Russian maneuvers were an open book. And of course, the civilian-population based, human-intelligence network also played a key role by providing accurate and timely information for the rebels about Russian locations and movements.

---

[455] Oliker, *Russia's Chechen Wars 1994-2000*, 20.

E. EXTERNAL FACTORS

The first important external factor in this case is the fact that, initially, the Chechens not only tailored their irregular strategy to the rough natural terrain and severe weather conditions of Chechnya, but they created an "urban terrain" that best supported their swarming strategy. "The Chechens simply applied their mastery at the art of forest warfare, so evident in the 18th and 19th centuries, to the urban forests in Grozny and other cities."[456] The Chechens had prepared for the Russian invasion for a long time and turned the country into a fortified battlefield to decrease the effectiveness of Russian weapons while increasing the lethality of their own. They many times locked down the first floors of buildings by blocking the doors, or booby-trapped the entrance around their ambush sites, to prevent the Russians from taking cover. The Chechens made use of the sewer systems as concealed avenues of approach and escape. Based

[456] Cassidy, Russia in Afghanistan and Chechnya, 44.

on their experiences in the Russian military, they could foresee possible assembly areas for ground forces and landing sites for Russian helicopters and could make preparations to increase the effectiveness of future attacks on those sites. "Moreover, the rebels had reinforced the basements and subbasements from which they fought, turning them into bunkers. Vaulted and sloped add-on roofs reduced the effects of Russian RPO-A Shmel flamethrowers and other systems."[457] Later, as the fight moved to mountainous areas of the country, the Chechens used physical features to their advantage, exploiting the limited number of roads and mountain passes as areas where they could lay effective ambushes against Russian armored convoys. The weather also had a significant influence on military operations, because the Russians knew surprisingly little about the Chechen climate. Especially the winter months had a significant effect on both the Russian soldiers and their equipment. Many of them did not have proper

---

[457] Oliker, Russia's Chechen Wars 1994-2000, 20.

clothing, and their vehicles were not prepared for functioning in a hard winter environment. Russian drivers frequently stayed in their vehicles with running engines, with which not only gave away their locations, but also burned a large amount of fuel.[458] The severe weather, including snow, low cloud cover, and fog, which is common in the mountains of Chechnya even during the summer months, was a key natural asset at the rebels' disposal. It sometimes restricted the Russian air force's support of ground troops and conduct of aerial reconnaissance, which provided temporal and local advantages for the rebels.[459]

The next significant external factor was the social terrain on both sides. On one hand, the

---

[458] Timothy L. Thomas, "The Caucasus conflict and Russian security: The Russian armed forces confront Chechnya III. The battle for Grozny, 1–26 January 1995," *The Journal of Slavic Military Studies*, Volume 10 Issue 1, 1997, 69, accessed March 09, 2012, http://www.tandfonline.com/doi/pdf/10.1080/1351804970843 0276.

[459] Faurby and Magnusson, "The Battle(s) of Grozny," 78.

intervention in Chechnya was not a popular decision in Russia. Not only was society divided on the question, but Russian leadership was as well. Some high ranking military leaders, including the deputy minister of defense, Boris Gromov, even went so far as to oppose the invasion. Others, like Colonel General Aleksey Mityukin, the commander of the northern Caucasus military district, refused to take command of the invading forces.[460] This division among Russian leadership played into the hands of the Chechen irregulars, who formed their psychological warfare strategy around it.

The social terrain had another significant aspect that influenced the outcome of the conflict. As Faurby and Magnusson explain, "The Russian leaders had no understanding of Chechen society. They had no understanding of the popular support for Chechen independence. They did not understand that as soon as Russian troops crossed into the republic, the majority of Chechens would put their

---

[460] Faurby and Magnusson, "The Battle(s) of Grozny," 83.

internal disagreements aside and fight under Dudayev as their symbol of national independence."[461] At the beginning of the invasion, even those Chechens who earlier opposed Dudayev immediately joined him in order to defend their independence. Without any indigenous allies, the Russians had no basis for any kind of cultural sensitivity or for a "local" force not seen by the civilian population as invaders. Simply put, the Russians had no chance to normalize the security situation through an ally. Furthermore, the Russians' continuous harassment of Chechen civilians and their indiscriminate aerial and artillery bombardments, which had no serious military effects on the rebel forces, deepened the anti-Russian mindset, which led to the majority of the taips being willing to provide fighters, supplies, and safe havens for the irregular forces. Since the Russians only controlled the rural areas temporarily, the support of the local taips allowed the Chechens

---

[461] Faurby and Magnusson, "The Battle(s) of Grozny," 84.

to rest and to refit their forces before sending them back into the fight. Since the Russians could never properly seal the borders of Chechnya, the rebels could also sneak to surrounding countries for medical treatment, weapons, and ammunitions, or to conduct raids deep into Russia.

The last external factor worth considering is the international environment in which the conflict occurred. Russian leadership was divided over the issue of Chechnya; from the rest of the world's point of view, including the American, it seemed straightforward. Only five years after the end of the Cold War, neither Washington nor other Western countries were willing to jeopardize their improving relationships with Russia over the issue of Chechnya. As President Clinton stated at a press conference in August 1994, his administration saw the events in Chechnya as an internal affair of Russia, which he hoped would be solved quickly and with minimal violence. This announcement "sent the message that the United States had no intention of involving itself in the conflict,"[462]whic h quickly made the Chechens realize that they could not hope for involvement by the US or other Western nations, unlike their covert support during the Russo–Afghan War. As a result of this, the Chechens fought a two-year war against a superior enemy without any significant outside support.

F. CHAPTER SUMMARY AND CONCLUSION

The centuries-old struggle between Russia and Chechnya arrived at a new chapter in the winter of 1994. After a couple of years of failed covert efforts, the Russian leadership, as it had so many times before, decided to use full-scale military intervention to restore law and order in, as they saw it, a rogue region. Russia deployed an overwhelming conventional military power against the small republic, but after less than two years of war, her forces were defeated and forced to

---

[462] Elizabeth Bagot, "US Ambivalence and the Russo-Chechen Wars: Behind the Silence," *Stanford Journal of International Relations*, Vol. XI No. 1, 2009, 33, accessed March 09, 2012, http://www.stanford.edu/group/sjir/pdf/Chechnya_11.1.pdf.

withdraw from Chechnya. This unexpected and remarkable success of a small state against a highly superior enemy was a result of the Chechens' understanding that they could not fight a war against the Russians on conventional terms, as any conventional strategy would have led to certain defeat. Based on this understanding, they chose to follow a swarming-based, irregular strategy, which proved to be highly effective and resulted in victory. There were several key factors that contributed to the success of the Chechen strategy.

First, the Chechen passion for independence, paired with national pride, brought the people of Chechnya together against the Russians. While the aggressor failed to get significant and legitimate indigenous support, Dudayev even managed to ally with his former opposition, who lined up on his side once the Russians crossed the border of their beloved country. His success in creating a single national will to resist a common outside enemy led to strong popular support for the rebels throughout the entire war. This support ensured continuous information superiority and human and material resupply for the rebels, which were key contributors for their success.

Second, large number of Chechen fighters, from the enlisted level to general officers, had gone through training in the Soviet/Russian military and many of them had previous combat experience, which an ad-hoc civilian militia would not commonly have had. From the first days of the war, these fighters were capable of effectively fighting, not only at the individual level, but at the unit level as well. They had the ability to understand irregular strategy and what the commander's intent required from them in best serving that strategy. As a result of their training, the rebels also knew Russian doctrine. They knew the Russian organizations, maneuver formations, unit-level tactics, and the strength and weaknesses of their weapon systems. The majority of the Chechens spoke Russian, and because of this, they could understand everything the Russians were communicating through their channels, which gave them a huge information advantage, allowing them to intercept radio messages and broadcast conflicting orders, which many times created not only chaos among the Russian troops, but high levels of casualties as the Russians were directed into Chechen ambushes.

The third key factor was the perfect symbiosis of the Chechen forces' network type organization, their weapons' "combined arms" effect at the small-unit level, and the tactics used by the irregular forces. The flat and decentralized organization was properly designed to fit the requirements of their irregular strategy and to exploit all the above-mentioned Chechen advantages. Their hundreds of small units had the ability to operate individually or, when the situation required joining forces temporarily, for specific operations. Their flexibility and lethality were increased by their combination of different weapon systems, which were employed with high effectiveness against carefully selected targets. Though the Chechens many times used traditional guerrilla-type, hit-and-run operations, they also took a step further by effectively integrating, in time and space, deliberate attacks on larger Russian formations, psychological warfare, and terrorism. The combination of these three factors presented military challenges that the Russian conventional strategy could not deal with.

Fourth, the Chechens knew and understood better the military applications of the physical features of their country. While designing their irregular strategy, they not only counted on the advantages of the terrain and weather, but made some serious pre-conflict preparations to create a "manmade wilderness" in their urban areas. The main goal of this infrastructure preparation was to enhance the effectiveness of irregular operations while taking away the strength of the Russian conventional forces.

The First Russo–Chechen War was chosen as a case study in this project because it provides one of the closest real-world examples of the theory of this thesis. Though the Chechen forces were not trained specifically for irregular warfare, they possessed most of the key elements of a proposed professional, irregular, homeland-defense force. Though after gaining their independence, the Chechen leadership considered establishing a conventional homeland-defense force, they quickly realized that that would never give them a chance for success against their possible future enemy, the numerically and technically superior Russian military. To be able to deal with the Russian threat, Chechen leaders introduced an irregular homeland-defense strategy. To have even a slight chance of success, the Chechens needed to unify the nation in support of an irregular strategy, which they did. Their new approach required a fundamentally different military organization and a much wider variety of tactics than the conventional mindset would have suggested. The Chechens organized their defensive forces into hundreds of small, independent units characterized by decentralized command and control and high organizational flexibility. The majority of the rebel fighters had pre-conflict military training and many had combat experience, which made them more effective than an ad-hoc civil militia would have been. Beyond their training, the rebels had an extensive knowledge of the enemy's doctrine and weapon systems. The Chechens also conducted significant infrastructural preparations prior to the war to further support the effectiveness of their operations. As a result of the effective integration and employment of all these factors, this far-off struggle between direct and indirect strategies ended with the remarkable victory of the small state, which is the reason why the First Russo–Chechen War "will be studied for ages by all military professionals."[463]

All this said, it is important to note that the Russians returned to Chechnya in 1999 to reassert their control. Before this second war, they made significantly different preparations by training and restructuring their forces for irregular war.[464] During the two-year conflict, Russian forces operated in small teams and used some of the

[463] Arquilla, *Insurgents, Raiders and Bandits*, 266.
[464] Oliker, *Russia's Chechen Wars 1994-2000*, 36-37.

Chechens' irregular methods against them. Their success in the second war, however, does not invalidate the irregular strategy. Instead, the Russians' improvements along irregular lines affirm the power of this approach.

CHAPTER 8

THE SECOND LEBANESE WAR

A. BACKGROUND

Following the quick defeat of Arab forces
by Israel during the Six-Day War in 1967,
Palestinian militants frequently launched cross-
border operations from southern Lebanon into the
northern parts of Israel. Many Arabs believed that
"guerrilla action...could 'redeem the honor of the
Arabs', which the regular armies had so
disgracefully lost."[465] As an eventual response to
these attacks, Israel briefly invaded Lebanon in
1978 and returned again in 1982, in Operation
Peace for Galilee. The second time, Israel kept its
forces in Lebanon until 2000, in order to destroy
Arab militant groups. Although Israeli forces
managed to expel the Palestine Liberation
Organization (the group mainly responsible for
attacks on Israel) from Lebanon their departure led

---

[465] Helena Cobban, *The Making of Modern Lebanon*,
(Boulder: Westview Press, 1985), 62.

to the establishment of a new, Shi`a-based militant group, Hezbollah, which means "party of God." This extremist organization, inspired by Ayatollah Khomeini, the leader of the 1979 Iranian revolution, enjoyed the support of Iran; and meanwhile, Syria declared war against Israel. Hezbollah`s initial objectives consisted of four major elements: continuous struggle against Israel until its destruction, forcing the withdrawal of foreign troops from Lebanon,[466] the liberation of Jerusalem, and the establishment of an Islamic state in Lebanon.[467]

Besides low-level harassing attacks against Israeli forces, Hezbollah`s early years were mainly characterized by terrorist acts. The organization

---

[466] A multinational peacekeeping force, including US Marines, French, and Italian troops, was deployed by the U.N. on 21 August 1982 to oversee the PLO withdrawal from Lebanon.

[467] David E. Johnson,"Minding the Middle: Insights from Hezbollah and Hamas for Future Warfare," *Strategic Insights*, Volume 10, Special Issue, October 2011, 125, accessed 22 March 2012, http://www.nps.edu/Academics/Centers/CCC/Research-Publications/StrategicInsights/2011/Oct/SI-v10-FoW_pg124-137_Johnson.pdf.

used a wide variety of methods in an effect to reach its objectives, including vehicle-borne suicide attacks, most notably those on the American embassy, United States Marine Corps barracks, and French paratrooper barracks in Beirut in 1983. In these attacks, Hezbollah killed 241 American servicemen and 58 French soldiers, while wounding an additional several hundred people. Beyond these suicide operations, the organization also kidnapped at least 51 foreign citizens between 1983 and 1986, including a French journalist, Roger Auque, and hijacked numerous airplanes.[468] Hezbollah quickly succeeded in forcing the withdrawal of French and American troops from Lebanese soil, and in 2000 Israel was pressured into moving its forces out of Lebanon as well. The permanent removal of the PLO and the Amal movement`s loss of a popular base[469] contributed to the fact that, by this time,

[468] Ronen Bergman, *The Secret War with Iran*, (New York: Free Press, 2008), 71-93.

[469] The Amal movement was founded in 1975 and became the most significant Shi`a militia during the Lebanese Civil War (1975-1990). Many Hezbollah members started their "carrier" in the Amal movement, including Secretary

Hezbollah was carrying out 90 percent of the operations against Israel and many Arabs believed that it became the "the sole party to conduct the struggle against Israel."[470] This enabled Hezbollah to "become the dominant military and political force in Lebanon."[471] The organization's influence was especially strong in the southern part of Lebanon, where Hezbollah slowly became a "state within the state."

Following Israel's withdrawal from Lebanon in 2000, Hezbollah, with the support of Iran, transformed itself into a social, media, and political organization while further developing its military capabilities. Between 2000 and 2006, Hezbollah trained thousands of fighters in various methods of

---

General Hassan Nasrallah. After 2000 the Hezbollah outgrew the Amal movement and took its place as the most significant Shi'a representing group in Lebanon.
Judith Palmer Harik, *Hezbollah: The Changing Face of Terrorism*, (New York: I. B. Tauris, 2004), 29-39.

[470] Nizar A. Hamzeh, "Lebanon's Hizbullah: from Islamic Revolution to Parliamentary
Accommodation," *Third World Quarterly*, Vol 14, No 2, 1993, accessed 22 March 2012,
http://ddc.aub.edu.lb/projects/pspa/hamzeh2.html.

[471] Bergman, *The Secret War with Iran*, 72.

irregular warfare, imported thousands of short- and long-range missiles, and built a well-fortified defense line in the southern areas to prepare for war with Israel. From 2005, Hezbollah introduced a new tactic into its repertoire: the kidnapping of Israeli soldiers. However, these operations usually concluded with prisoner exchanges between the two parties. The situation changed on 12 July 2006, when Hezbollah ambushed an Israeli border patrol, killed three Israeli reservists, and kidnapped two soldiers.[472] After a failed rescue attempt, during which five more Israeli soldiers were killed and a tank destroyed, the Israeli government decided to respond with greater force to this event. This decision triggered a 34-day war that not only highlighted several problems within the conventionally minded Israeli defense forces, but once again demonstrated the power of irregular warfare.

Even before the official decision was made to go to war, the Israeli air force was already

---

[472] Farquhar, *Back to Basics,* 6.

extensively deployed. In the early morning of July 13, it attacked and destroyed about 50 of Hezbollah's known long-range missile sites within 34 minutes. The Israeli Air Force also targeted "Hezbollah observation posts along the border, Hezbollah compounds in the *Dahyia* section of Beirut, and roads and bridges that Israel believed might be used to exfiltrate the abducted soldiers."[473] As a response to these air attacks, Hezbollah started to launch rockets into Israel, hitting mainly urban areas. The steady flow of these rockets throughout the entire conflict claimed 53 Israeli civilian lives and showed the Israeli government that air attacks by themselves could not destroy Hezbollah's offensive capabilities. To deal with the rocket threat, the Israelis started a major ground offensive on July 19, but met much tougher resistance than they expected, especially around Marun ar Ras and

---

[473] Stephen Biddle and Jeffrey A. Friedman, *The 2006 Lebanon Campaign and the Future of the Warfare: Implications for Army and Defense Policy*, (Carlisle: Strategic Studies Institute, 2008), 30, accessed 23 March 2012, file:///D:/thesis%20literature/lebanon%20war/The%202006%20Lebanon%20Campaign%20and%20the%20Future%20of%20Warfare%20%20Impl ications%20for%20Army%20and%20De.

Bint Jbeil. To protect its launch sites and weapons caches, Hezbollah designed a defensive system "based on underground tunnels and bunkers, explosives-ridden areas, and anti-tank units. This array was intended to confront ground forces to a limited extent, to stall ground incursions, and inflict as many casualties as possible, which would wear out IDF forces, slow down their progress, and allow continued rocket fire."[474]

The initial Israeli strategy did not aim at controlling the ground, but only on destroying launch sites and missiles. But when its ineffectiveness became clear by July 31, the "Israeli Cabinet approved 'Operation Change of Direction 8', designed to take and hold a security zone several kilometers wide along the entire border."[475] Eight additional Israeli brigades were deployed, and with these units, the number of Israeli forces increased to about 30,000. Within ten days, as a result of this operation, the Israelis had a footprint in almost

---

[474] Farquhar, *Back to Basics,* 8.

[475] Biddle and Friedman, *The 2006 Lebanon Campaign and the Future of the Warfare,* 32.

every Lebanese city in the border area, but everywhere they penetrated they found fierce Hezbollah defenses and paid a huge price for every kilometer taken. In these built-up areas, Hezbollah "integrated effective standoff weapons, such as antitank guided missiles (ATGMs), mortars, and short-range rockets, with mines and improvised explosive devices (IEDs) and competent fighters."[476] This presented a complicated challenge for the Israeli forces. Beyond the heavy urban fighting, Hezbollah's rockets continued to fall on Israeli territory, wounding and killing civilians. On 12 August, Israel launched an offensive to occupy Lebanese soil up to the Litani River. The next two days brought fierce fighting and caused a large number of casualties and material loss on both sides. For example, in the Israeli 401st Armored Brigade, eleven tanks were hit and twelve of its soldiers killed during their advance through the Saluqi Valley, while Hezbollah lost about fifty fighters. [477] On 14 August, both sides agreed to

---

[476] Johnson,"Minding the Middle," 126.

implement a United Nations Security Council ceasefire; and though some low-level incidents still occurred during the next couple days, the 34-day war between Israel and Hezbollah officially ended.

B. IRREGULAR STRATEGY

Hezbollah's ideology calls for the destruction of Israel, but the leadership of the Shi'a organization understood that it was highly unlikely for them to militarily destroy Israel or its forces in an open, conventional war. Although the leaders of Hezbollah did not anticipate so serious a response from Israel in 2006, they were still prepared for war. During the years between 2000 and 2006, Hezbollah planners continuously worked on a generic strategy that could be used in any future war against Israel. They knew that in case of conflict, Israel could occupy Lebanon again as it did in 1978 and 1982, and they could not stop it using conventional ways of defense. Based on this understanding, they needed to come up with a

---

[477] Biddle and Friedman, *The 2006 Lebanon Campaign and the Future of the Warfare*, 32-33.

strategy that either would deter Israel from an invasion, or in case of the failure of deterrence, coerce Israel into halting the offense and withdrawing forces from Lebanon.[478] The events following the killing of three, and kidnapping of two, Israeli soldiers on 12 July 2006 quickly made it clear that the deterrence part failed, so Hezbollah needed to put its coercive strategy into motion.

Hezbollah's irregular approach was designed around the basic assumption that Israeli society was highly sensitive to casualties and would not be able to tolerate "pain." In Hezbollah's mind, as Secretary-General Hassan Nasrallah explained, Israeli society was a "brittle post-military society that cannot endure wars anymore and that under pressure it can succumb to Arab aggression."[479] To inflict such pain and coerce Israeli society, it was paramount to Hezbollah's strategy to "penetrate well inside Israel's border and not yield to the IDF's

---

[478] Biddle and Friedman, *The 2006 Lebanon Campaign and the Future of the Warfare*, 52-53.

[479] Farquhar, *Back to Basics,* 7.

massive precision firepower."[480] Initially, long-range rocket systems seemed to be the best solution for Hezbollah to provide the coercive threat. Their locations, deep in Lebanon, placed them beyond the reach of ground attack, but as the success of the Israeli air force in the first day of the war demonstrated, their large footprints were too vulnerable to airstrikes. Hezbollah quickly recognized that to be successful, it had to rely on its shorter-range rocket systems and the capabilities of the fortified defensive lines established to protect those systems. Although these rockets provided much less threatening than long-range ones, they were "smaller, easier to conceal, vastly greater in number, and potentially much less vulnerable to aerial preemption."[481] Hezbollah realized that a complete denial of Israeli ground forces from the short-range rockets' launch sites would be impossible. But as a key requirement of success, they needed to buy time. As Biddle and Friedman

---

[480] Farquhar, *Back to Basics,* 7.

[481] Biddle and Friedman, *The 2006 Lebanon Campaign and the Future of the Warfare,* 49.

explain, it was necessary:

> ...to prevent the Israelis from getting quick access to the key launch areas on the scale needed to search the terrain exhaustively and uproot concealed rocket launchers before enough pressure could be built on the Israeli government to yield the issue at stake. This operational requirement could not be met with classical guerrilla tactics, which allow enemy forces into the country but gradually penalize them for their presence with hit-and-run casualty infliction.[482]

Based on this mindset, and understanding they could not stop the Israelis by employing a conventional defense, Hezbollah planners designed a ground-defense system that could buy time and allow "ongoing rocket fire in the meantime to inflict mounting coercive pain on Israeli society."[483] To increase the effectiveness of the missiles, Hezbollah units assigned to protect the rocket systems were organized into small, highly mobile and decentralized elements, which used swarming as

---

[482] Biddle and Friedman, *The 2006 Lebanon Campaign and the Future of the Warfare*, 51.

[483] Biddle and Friedman, *The 2006 Lebanon Campaign and the Future of the Warfare*, 50.

their main operational method. Hezbollah's fighters were well trained and most of them were veterans from the earlier eighteen-year (1982–2000) struggle against Israel. They were equipped with a wide range of weapon systems, including machine guns, anti-tank missiles, mortars, and sniper rifles, to increase effectiveness. Beyond all these factors, Hezbollah put a high emphasis on the preparation of engagement areas and kill zones along possible avenues of approach. "Mines and IEDs were expertly placed in depth throughout the southern defensive sector in order to stop Israeli mechanized forces and enable Hezbollah to mass both direct and indirect fires on their halted columns."[484] This defense system provided effective protection for rocket units and inflicted great casualties on the Israeli forces. Ron Tira, an Israeli air force officer, explained how the Israeli military leadership saw the essence of Hezbollah's strategy by stating "Hezbollah designed a war in which presumably Israel could only choose which soft underbelly to

---

[484] Farquhar, *Back to Basics,* 8.

expose: the one whereby it avoids a ground operation and exposes its home front vulnerability, or the one whereby it enters Lebanon and sustains the loss of soldiers in ongoing ground-based attrition with a guerrilla organization. Hezbollah's brilliant trap apparently left Israel with two undesirable options."[485]

Hezbollah also integrated effective media exploitation and psychological warfare into its irregular strategy to influence multiple audiences, including the organization's own followers, other Arab governments, and their populations. Israel's military forces and morale were targeted as well, in the hope of encouraging withdrawal from Lebanon. Finally, Hezbollah strove to convince the outside world to stop supporting Israel. Hezbollah used the mass media, including its own television station, called *al-Manar*, and the Internet, as key weapons

---

[485] Ron Tira, "Breaking the Amoeba's Bones," *Strategic Assessment*, Jaffee
Center for Strategic Studies, Tel Aviv University, Vol. 9, No. 3, November 2006, 9, accessed 24 March 2012,
http://www.inss.org.il/publications.php?cat=21&incat=&read=84.

against Israel. It could do so because during this conflict, so much information became available to the media that it changed journalism's role in future conflicts. As Marvin Kalb explained "once upon a time, such information was the stuff of military intelligence acquired with considerable efforts and risk; now it has become the stuff of everyday journalism. The camera and the computer have become weapons of war."[486] He added that the Internet in 2006 "helped produce the first really 'live' war in history."[487] As a key part of its media exploitation, Hezbollah used reporters of al-Manar as embedded assets to capture footage of the fighting and manipulate it as they saw it fit for overall strategic goals. Later this footage were broadcast in the region by al-Manar and Hezbollah's website and were also made available

---

[486] Marvin Kalb, "The Israeli-Hezbollah War of 2006: The Media As a Weapon in Asymmetrical Conflict" *Joan Shorenstein Center on the Press, Politics and Public Policy*, February 2007, 4, accessed 25 March 2012,http://www.ksg.harvard.edu/presspol/research_publicatio ns/papers/research_papers/R29.pdf.

[487] Kalb, "The Israeli-Hezbollah War of 2006," 4.

for foreign networks, including al-Jazeera and CNN.

Beyond the use of this footage, Hezbollah was also successful in making the Israeli forces believe that it had the capability to intercept their secret, frequency-hopping radio communications. However, research conducted after the war showed that this was another brilliant psychological warfare operation from Hezbollah. As David Fulghum explained in his article, *Doubt as a Weapon,*

> What they're really doing is a very good psychological operations...one of the things you want to do is instill doubt. Hezbollah makes the pronouncement that they can read encrypted radios. They wanted the IDF troops to believe they weren't as invulnerable as they thought. It ran like wildfire through the U.S. troops as well. What you're witnessing is unsophisticated technology exploited by sophisticated information operations. They scored big time in the psychological warfare department the enemy is figuring out ways to use the information age against us.[488]

---

[488] David Fulghum, "Doubt as a Weapon," *Aviation Week & Space Technology,*" 27 November 2006, 26.

The effective integration of all these factors enabled a small, state-within-a-state-like organization to effectively defend against a numerically and technologically superior enemy and force its withdrawal from Lebanese soil.

C. ORGANIZATION AND LEADERSHIP

By 2006, after decades of continual structural transformation, Hezbollah developed an organizational form that enabled it to be one of the significant ruling powers in Lebanon and to take on the characteristics of a "state" in the southern part of the country. At that time, Hezbollah`s organization resembled that of a political party, but it had its own military capabilities as well. The organization was, and currently is, led by the Supreme Shura Council, which consists of seventeen members. "The Supreme Shura Council is the highest authority in the party and is charged with legislative, executive, judicial, political, and military affairs and with the overall administration of the party."[489] Hezbollah`s daily operations are directed by the Secretary General, Sayyed Hassan Nasrallah and his deputy, Naim Qassem. Sayyed Hassan Nasrallah, who has been the leader of Hezbollah since 1992, is a proved guerrilla commander, a powerful leader, and skilled propagandist committed to Israel's destruction and the establishment of an Islamist state in Lebanon.[490] He is seen by his followers as a messianic figure with more power than any Lebanese political official. He is also a member of the executive committee of Hezbollah. This committee consists of four districts, including Beirut, the southern suburbs, the south, and the Biq`a Valley, each with leaders of their own, and five additional members who are chosen by the Supreme Shura. Directly subordinated to the executive committee one can find the politburo, with fifteen members who do not have decision-making authority; rather they coordinate and supervise the activities of the three

---

[489] Hamzeh, "Lebanon's Hizbullah."

[490] Kaplan, Eben, "Profile: Hassan Nasrallah," Council on Foreign Relations, July 20, 2006, accessed 25 March 2012, http://www.cfr.org/publication/11132/profile.html.

sub-elements: the enforcement, recruitment, and propaganda; holy reconstruction; and security organs. During the 2006 conflict, all these sub-elements played a key role in Hezbollah`s success. The first had "a vital role in the reinforcement of Hezbollah's doctrines and contributed extensively to the mobilization of hundreds of young Shi'ites to the cause of Hezbollah."[491] The second provided "support services to members, new recruits, and supporters of Hezbollah. These services range from medical care to financial aid, housing, and public utilities."[492] The security organ had two main tasks: protecting the key leaders of Hezbollah and running effective intelligence gathering and counter-intelligence operations against Israeli intelligence services. All these sub-elements played an important supportive rule in the 2006 conflict, but the most important organizational unit was the fourth sub-element, the combat organ. As Nizar A. Hamzeh observes, this element originally consisted

---

[491] Hamzeh, "Lebanon's Hizbullah."
[492] Hamzeh, "Lebanon's Hizbullah."

of two parts: "the Islamic Resistance (al-Muqawamah al-Islamiyyah), and the Islamic Holy War (al-Jihad al-Islami). While the first one is in charge of suicide attacks against Western and Israeli targets, the second one led more conventional attacks against Israeli troops in the south."[493] In the Second Lebanese War, Hezbollah mainly relied on the Islamic holy war section. Based on Israeli intelligence estimates at that time, Hezbollah had about 10,000 fighters available, but they deployed about 3,000 of them, from the Nasser Brigade, south of the Litani River along Israel`s northern borders. Besides the conventional unit designation, none of the structural elements of this unit followed conventional military organizational principles.

Hezbollah units were organized into three major groups: short-range rocket crews, medium-range rocket crews, and light-infantry units. The first rocket teams were foot-and-bicycle mobile units consisting of lookouts, rocket transporters, and launching teams. After the lookouts declared an

---

[493] Hamzeh, "Lebanon's Hizbullah."

area clear, a second team transported the rockets to the launch site then left. Seconds later, the firing team arrived and launched the rocket. The medium-range rocket teams had larger weapon systems that required some type of transportation. The Fajr and extended-range Katyushas "were to be fired from vehicle-mounted launchers, often a pickup truck or the ubiquitous small flatbed farm trucks of the region."[494] Those fighters who were assigned to defend the rockets operated in small decentralized cells organized into direct and indirect fire teams. These small units were capable of conducting either hit-and-run attacks or positional defense by effectively massing direct and indirect fire on the advancing Israeli columns. Although all these organizational elements operated in a highly decentralized manner, as Biddle and Friedman explain:

> Hezbollah exercised a degree of
> hierarchical, differentiated command and
> control over subunits operating in key areas
> during the campaign, making apparent

---

[494] Farquhar, *Back to Basics*, 8.

decisions to favor some sectors over others, hold in some places but yield in others, counterattack in some locations but with draw elsewhere. A formal chain of command operated from designated and well-equipped command posts; used real-time communications systems including landline cables and encrypted radio; issued orders; changed plans; and moved some elite units over considerable distances from rearward reserve areas to reinforce the key battle for the communications network in the central sector.[495]

Hezbollah understood that the Israeli forces would follow a direct strategy, which would be based on the need to "achieve effects" on Hezbollah's system. To prevent this and to take away the advantages of the Israeli precision-weapon systems Hezbollah created a "network of autonomous cells with little inter-cell systemic interaction,"[496] which minimized their footprint and appearance time while providing maximum operational effectiveness. As Penny L. Mellies states,

---

[495] Biddle and Friedman, *The 2006 Lebanon Campaign and the Future of the Warfare,* 59.

[496] Farquhar, *Back to Basics,* 10.

"Hezbollah acted as a 'distributed network' of small cells and units acting with considerable independence, and capable of rapidly adapting to local conditions rather than having to react faster than the IDF's decision cycle, they could largely ignore it, waiting out Israeli attacks, staying in positions, reinfiltrating or reemerging from cover, and choosing the time to attack or ambush."[497]

D. INTERNAL FACTORS

One of the major internal factors that led to the success of Hezbollah in the Second Lebanese War was the high level of pre-conflict training and combat experience of its fighters in irregular-warfare methods. The eighteen-year struggle against Israel not only allowed Hezbollah to gain significant combat experience, but provided an opportunity to figure out the Israeli forces' doctrine and operational procedures. Based on their knowledge and understanding of the enemy, Hezbollah developed an effective counter strategy

---

[497] Farquhar, *Back to Basics,* 66.

and focused the training of its forces on the irregular character of the future war they expected to wage against Israel. Between 2000 and 2006, most of the Nasser Brigade received training in Iran and Syria, designed to provide the highest chance of success for Hezbollah's irregular approach. It included operating different weapon systems, conducting day and night operations, integrating direct and indirect fires, use of mines, and constructing of improvised, explosive devices.[498] One of the examples of the effective integration of pre-conflict experience and training was the capability of short-range rocket units to set up a launch site and fire a rocket within 28 seconds, during which time they could prevent Israeli forces from conducting an attack on the site.[499]

The next significant internal factor that made Hezbollah's resistance so effective was the type of tactics it used during the war. Hezbollah employed not only a unique combination of traditional

---

[498] Bergman, *The Secret War with Iran*, 256-257.
[499] Farquhar, *Back to Basics,* 8.

guerrilla type hit-and-run tactics and swarming, but like the Chechens showed remarkable ability and willingness to engage in long firefights both in defense and on offense against larger Israeli formations. As Penny L. Mellies observes, Hezbollah tactics included "indirect fire attacks, primarily with rocket and mortar; direct fire attacks (anti-armor and surface-to-air fire), employed explosives, IEDs/explosively-formed penetrator (EFP) and mines, and conducted raids, ambushes and kidnappings."[500] In offense, Hezbollah relied heavily on its indirect fire capabilities and ambushes. The rockets' concealment in urban areas and well-prepared caches and the ability of units to set up launch sites quickly, fire rockets, and melt back into the "terrain" without detection, provided significant operational advantages to Hezbollah. Ambushes, especially those conducted with guided anti-tank missiles, on advancing Israeli troop columns, were very effective as well. In the already mentioned example of the Israeli 401st Brigade,

---

[500] Farquhar, *Back to Basics,* 61.

eleven tanks were hit and twelve soldiers killed by Hezbollah's fire during an ambush.[501] Tough attacks on the advancing Israeli troops were frequent. Many times Hezbollah would "allow IDF troops to pass its fighters hiding in 'nature reserves' and other places, and then continue surface-to-surface rocket fire into Israel and guerilla operations against rearguard forces. Thus, any Israeli movement deep into Lebanese territory had to include a thorough sweep to secure all the built-up and open areas taken by the IDF."[502] As Matt M. Matthews notes "Hezbollah's tactical proficiency bewildered the IDF. Hezbollah was not simply hunkering down and defending terrain but was using its small-arms, mortars, rockets, and antitank weapons to successfully maneuver against the IDF."[503]

On defense, Hezbollah used its prepared and well-concealed strong points and fortified defensive positions with high effectiveness. As a unique

---

[501] Biddle and Friedman, *The 2006 Lebanon Campaign and the Future of the Warfare*, 32.

[502] Tira, "Breaking the Amoeba's Bones."

[503] Farquhar, *Back to Basics,* 15.

difference from traditional guerrilla tactics, Hezbollah fighters, most of them wearing clearly identifiable military uniforms, did not avoid long-lasting firefights in an effort to preserve their forces. It happened on numerous occasions that firefights lasting several hours took place between the parties while Hezbollah fighters tried to hold key positions. An example of such an engagement happened at the Shaked outpost. "A dug-in Hezbollah defensive position remained in place on a critical hillcrest near the Israeli border between Avivim and Marun ar Ras, exchanging fire with IDF tanks and infantry for more than 12 hours before finally being destroyed in place by Israeli fire."[504] The other unique factor of Hezbollah's fighting style was that its fighters continued to engage Israeli forces at close range and in many cases they did not even try to break contact or withdraw, as guerrillas would have done. Hezbollah's units occasionally also conducted squad and platoon size counterattacks as

---

[504] Biddle and Friedman, *The 2006 Lebanon Campaign and the Future of the Warfare*, 35.

well. In one case, between fifteen and 30 fighters assaulted an Israeli company position with the objective of recapturing Hill 951. In another case, about 60 Hezbollah members attacked an Israeli position on Hill 850. In both operations, the attackers were divided into two major, conventional-style elements: a main effort, assaulting the hill, and a supporting effort, providing guided anti-tank missile and mortar support from at least two directions.[505]

These above described kinetic tactics were effectively integrated with information operations (IO). Hezbollah employed experts in "psychological warfare and propaganda, operating its own television, radio, and internet sites and collaborating with supporting media."[506] Hezbollah's information-warfare strategy was focused on highlighting the vulnerabilities of Israeli society and military forces while continuously presenting its own battlefield successes, the suffering of Lebanese

---

[505] Biddle and Friedman, *The 2006 Lebanon Campaign and the Future of the Warfare*, 39.

[506] Farquhar, *Back to Basics*, 66.

people, and the collateral damage caused by Israeli operations. "Hezbollah accomplished this by performing sophisticated editing and photo and video manipulation, presenting a skewed picture of the war's progress."[507] The most shocking media exploitation conducted by Hezbollah took place on July 14, 2006 when Secretary-General Hassan Nasrallah appeared on al-Manar and presented a "live countdown" to a missile strike conducted against the INS *Hanit*. As the two C-802 anti-ship missiles were launched, "he confidently suggested that viewers in Beirut look toward the west for a spectacular sight. The timing of the broadcast was impeccable and serving as a lethal theatrical drum roll."[508] This was just one of the numerous examples of how Hezbollah used information operations as a combat multiplier.

The effectiveness of Hezbollah kinetic tactics and information operations were enabled by the ability to sustain a reliable communication

[507] Farquhar, *Back to Basics,* 66.
[508] Farquhar, *Back to Basics,* 65.

system throughout the entire conflict. It had "excellent, diverse, and hard-to-target C2 capabilities included fiber-optic landlines, cell phones, secure radio, messengers, the internet and the *al-Manar* television station."[509] The extent of Hezbollah's communication capabilities became clear in the implementation of the ceasefire. As Crooke and Perry explain, the fact that the organization's leaders easily enforced the agreement on their unit commanders proved that:

> Hezbollah's communication's capabilities had survived Israel's air onslaught, that the Hezbollah leadership was in touch with its commanders on the ground, and that those commanders were able to maintain a robust communications network despite Israeli interdiction. More simply, Hezbollah's ability to cease fire meant that Israel's goal of separating Hezbollah fighters from their command structure (considered a necessity by modern armies in waging a war on a sophisticated technological battlefield) had failed.[510]

---

[509] Farquhar, *Back to Basics,* 61.

[510] Alastair Crooke and Mark Perry, "How Hezbollah Defeated Israel,Part 1: Winning the intelligence war," *Asia Times*, 12 Octorber 2006, accessed 25 March 2012,

88

888

The last internal factor that had a significant influence on the end results of the Second Lebanese War was the role of intelligence. During the conflict, Hezbollah had significant advantages in this area, based on the unique integration of the knowledge of the Israeli forces` procedures and three additional factors: Hezbollah`s military deception operations, its counter-intelligence operations before the war, and its tight operational security within. As part of its deception strategy, Hezbollah presented numerous "dummy" bunkers and launch sites to provide a "target-reach" battlefield for the conventionally minded Israeli military leadership. Several bunkers were "constructed in the open and often under the eyes of Israeli drone vehicles or under the observation of Lebanese citizens with close ties to the Israelis."[511] Meanwhile it built its real fortified positions, which were expertly camouflaged, in areas that were hidden even from

http://www.atimes.com/atimes/Middle_East/HJ12Ak01.html.
[511] Crooke and Perry, "How Hezbollah Defeated Israel."

the Lebanese population. The effectiveness of Hezbollah's deception was further increased by its ability to turn many Israeli agents, and through them to feed false information back into the Israeli intelligence system. Thus when the attacking Israeli forces entered Lebanon, most of their intelligence was false and they paid a huge price for it.[512] As one of the Israeli soldiers explained "we expected a tent and three Kalashnikovs—that was the intelligence we were given. Instead, we found a hydraulic steel door leading to a well-equipped network of tunnels."[513] Finally, Hezbollah's ability to control information internally provided a significant advantage and restricted Israeli intelligence access to critical operational information. As Crooke and Perry write,

> For security reasons, no single commander knew the location of each bunker and each distinct Hezbollah militia unit was assigned access to three bunkers only - a

---

[512] Crooke and Perry, "How Hezbollah Defeated Israel."
[513] Farquhar, *Back to Basics,* 15.

primary munitions bunker and two reserve
bunkers, in case the primary bunker was
destroyed… The security protocols for the
marshaling of troops were diligently
maintained. No single Hezbollah member
had knowledge of the militia's entire
bunker structure.[514]

The mutually supporting combination of these
intelligence functions and their integration into
Hezbollah`s overall strategy was an important
enabler for final success.

E. EXTERNAL FACTORS

The effective use of natural terrain and its
augmentation with well built and concealed
defensive positions were key elements in
Hezbollah`s strategy. The defenders recognized and
exploited those areas of south Lebanon that had
military usefulness and possible advantages over the
attackers. Urban areas, having important road
junctions and operationally key terrain features,
were fortified and heavily defended, while, for

---

[514] Crooke and Perry, "How Hezbollah Defeated Israel."

example, the southwestern part of Lebanon had much less defensible terrain and was defended only temporarily and with lighter forces. As Biddle and Friedman state, "villages near the border with Israel were systematically better prepared for defense and more strongly manned than those in the interior. Supplies and ammunition were stockpiled in locations commanding key terrain; other positions appear to have received little logistical prepositioning."[515] For its short- and medium-range rocket systems, Hezbollah built launch sites "into the ground, using pneumatic lifts to raise and lower the launchers from underground shelters. Many were launched from trucks positioned as standalone launchers. Firing teams sought protection in nearby bunkers and caves to hide from IDF counter-battery attacks."[516] Crooke and Perry find that "the most important command bunkers and weapons-arsenal bunkers were dug deeply into Lebanon's rocky hills - to a depth of 40 meters.

---

[515] Biddle and Friedman, *The 2006 Lebanon Campaign and the Future of the Warfare*, 58.

[516] Farquhar, *Back to Basics,* 63.

Nearly 600 separate ammunition and weapons bunkers were strategically placed in the region south of the Litani."[517] All the above described pre-conflict battlefield-preparation efforts conducted by Hezbollah effectively supported its strategy during the conflict and served as an important force multiplier against a numerically and technologically superior enemy. As Penny L. Mellies states, "Hezbollah's ability to exploit virtually any built up area and familiar terrain as fortresses or ambush sites at least partially compensated for IDF armor, air mobility, superior firepower, and sensors."[518]

Beyond the natural and manmade terrain, the social environment also played a key role in the conflict. In the previous cases, as a significant part of the irregular struggle, the fighting usually took place in close proximity to the civilian population, which enabled the rebel forces to melt back into the civilian society after their operations, thus to avoid

---

[517] Crooke and Perry, "How Hezbollah Defeated Israel."
[518] Farquhar, *Back to Basics,* 62.

detection. Hezbollah enjoyed strong popular support in south Lebanon, especially among the Shi`a population, but it did not use civilian society as a "hiding place" in a significant way during the Second Lebanese War. It is also important to note that Hezbollah did not extend its defensive infrastructure to those areas populated mainly by Christians. The lack of a supportive population in those areas made it impossible to keep Hezbollah's war preparations hidden from Israeli intelligence. Hezbollah was blamed for using civilians as human shields, and did indeed use residential buildings to hide fighting positions and rocket-launch sites, but the vast majority of civilians were evacuated from the area in the wake of the conflict. Furthermore, Hezbollah fighters, with few exceptions, wore clearly distinguishable military uniforms and so tried to melt into the civilian population only on rare occasions. As Biddle and Friedman explained,

> The key battlefields in the land campaign south of the Litani River were mostly devoid of civilians, and IDF participants consistently report little or no meaningful intermingling of Hezbollah fighters and

noncombatants. Nor is there any systematic reporting of Hezbollah using civilians in the combat zone as shields. The fighting in southern Lebanon was chiefly urban, in the built-up areas of the small to medium-size villages and towns typical of the region. But it was not significantly intermingled with a civilian population that had fled by the time the ground fighting began. [519]

The last significant external factor that played a key role in the success of Hezbollah`s irregular strategy was the international environment in which the conflict took place. During the preparation for conflict, Hezbollah received significant support from three countries. Between 2000 and 2006, Iran and Syria provided financial support for infrastructure preparation, supplied Hezbollah with a large amount of modern Iranian, Russian, and Chinese weapon systems, and provided training for thousands of Hezbollah fighters. Iranian Revolutionary Guard officers and North Korean "defensive guerrilla warfare" experts

---

[519] Biddle and Friedman, *The 2006 Lebanon Campaign and the Future of the Warfare*, 43-44.

participated in designing and building Hezbollah's defensive system. As Matt M. Matthews states, "all the underground facilities [Hezbollah's], including arms dumps, food stocks, dispensaries for the wounded, were put in place primarily in 2003-2004 under the supervision of North Korean instructors. Evidence would further suggest that the Iranian Revolutionary Guard was also heavily involved in the construction effort."[520] During the actual conflict, Iran continued to supply Hezbollah with rockets and other weapons, and also provided significant intelligence support as well. Some sources even suggest that Hezbollah's Secretary-General Hassan Nasrallah took refuge and commanded the entire war from the Iranian Embassy in Beirut.[521]

Not surprisingly, Israel's traditional allies, including the United States, the United Kingdom, and Germany, supported Israel's right to defend itself and the US even authorized the immediate

---

[520] Farquhar, *Back to Basics,* 9.
[521] Crooke and Perry, "How Hezbollah Defeated Israel."

shipment of precision-guided bombs to increase the effectiveness of Israeli forces,[522] which ironically further strengthened the IDF`s proponents of the conventional solution to the conflict and played right into Hezbollah`s hands. Several Arab countries, including Egypt and Jordan, also heavily criticized Hezbollah`s actions and called on the U.N. to interfere to stop the fighting. Initially this request did not find any support within the Security Council, since the US and UK trusted that Israel would win and hoped for a final blow to be delivered against Hezbollah. But it soon became evident that Hezbollah would not be defeated quickly and easily. This recognition finally led to the unanimous approval of U.N. Security Council Resolution 1701, which ended the 34-day war between Hezbollah and Israel.

---

[522] David S. Cloud, "U.S. Speeds Up Bomb Delivery for the Israelis," *New York Times*, 22 July 2006, accessed 28 March 2012, http://www.nytimes.com/2006/07/22/world/middleeast/22milit ary.html?pagewanted=all.

F. CHAPTER SUMMARY AND CONCLUSION

In 2000, after eighteen years of transformation and adaptation, Hezbollah drove Israel from southern Lebanon and became a state within a state. The organization not only functioned as a political entity and provided social services to Lebanon`s population, but acted as a state would have done in preparing to prevent future Israeli occupation. Before the conflict started, Hezbollah, with the help of foreign sponsors, spent six years preparing its forces in South Lebanon for war. And though it came as a surprise, the war found Hezbollah better prepared and able to fight more effectively than anyone would have thought. During its preparation, Hezbollah designed a unique strategy that best fitted its ideology, goals, operational environment, and available resources, and proved to be successful against Israel. There were several key factors that contributed to the unexpected success of Hezbollah during the war.

Since Hezbollah had fought against Israel

for eighteen years, its planners and fighters thoroughly knew their enemy's thinking, procedures, capabilities of their weapons systems, etc. Based on this knowledge, Hezbollah built a military force before the war that best supported its strategy. This military force was specifically structured and trained for irregular warfare, and was not an ad hoc raised force, organized after a conventional defeat. The essence of the organization of Hezbollah`s forces were explained by Anthony H. Cordesman in his book, *Lessons of the 2006 Israeli-Hezbollah War*, as follows:

> Hezbollah further organized its fighters into small, self-sufficient teams capable of operating independently and without direction from high authority for long periods of time. Although an elaborate system of radio call signs, a closed cellular phone system, and two-way radios allowed these teams to stay in touch with their higher units, a great level of wartime decision-making leeway was given to the junior ranks, largely mitigating the need for such communications....As for its counterparts in Chechnya, Iraq, and Afghanistan, Hezbollah's looser structure may have worked to its distinct advantage during the

2006 war, allowing units the flexibility necessary for quick reaction and adjustment to Israeli offensives.[523]

Secretary-General Hassan Nasrallah also explained Hezbollah's 'new model' army by stating "it was not a regular army but was not a guerrilla in the traditional sense either. It was something in between."[524]

To further increase the effectiveness of this new model army, Hezbollah conducted extensive infrastructure preparation in south Lebanon. The construction and sophisticated concealment of fortified positions, tunnel systems, and large caches of hidden, pre-positioned weapons, in combination with the unique integration of conventional tactics and irregular methods, completely threw the Israeli forces off balance and severely reduced their technological and numerical advantages. Hezbollah's strategy focused on defense, but its

---

[523] Anthony H. Cordesman, *Lessons of the 2006 Israeli-Hezbollah War*, (Washington D. C.: Center for Strategic and International Studies, 2007) 80-81.

[524] Farquhar, *Back to Basics,* 9.

uniqueness and effectiveness enabled it to seize and hold the initiative at times throughout the entire war. As Andrew Exum stated, "this was a very good lesson in asymmetric warfare. This was not Israel imposing its battle on Hezbollah but Hezbollah imposing its battle on Israel."[525] But not only were the physical environment prepared and the kinetic operations effectively integrated, the successful use of psychological warfare and media exploitation were also key elements.

Hezbollah properly recognized the military value of the media and entered the war with an already functioning system. Through its own television station, its web site, and the use of embedded reporters, Hezbollah retained its ability during the entire conflict to formulate and communicate its agenda to the proper target audiences, which had a significant impact on the end results of the conflict.

---

[525] Andrew Exum, *Hizballah at War. A Military Assessment*, (Washington D.C.: Washington Institute for Near East Policy, 2006) 5, accessed on 02 April 2012, http://www.lebanonwire.com/0701MLN/Hezbollah_at_war.pdf.

Finally, the information advantage possessed by Hezbollah also played a paramount role in the outcome of the conflict. Hezbollah`s advantages could be found in four major areas. First, it had an extensive knowledge on Israeli military doctrine, while Israel operated on the bases of wrong assumptions by expecting the same type of fighting from Hezbollah as it had before. Second, through "turned" agents, Hezbollah managed to feed the Israelis false information. Third, by expertly concealing its positions and using many dummy bunkers, Hezbollah misled Israeli intelligence, especially its aerial platforms, regarding its defensive structures. Fourth, the ability to sustain extreme information security within the organization denied the Israelis access to key information during the conflict. All these elements acted as force multipliers for the irregulars, since they not only helped hide their operations, but also exposed the invading Israeli forces to counterattack.

The Second Lebanese War was chosen as a case study in this project because Hezbollah's strategy, force structure, training, infrastructure preparation, and type of operations provide the closest real-world example of the proposed theory of this thesis. As a result of Hezbollah`s effective combination of ancient irregular methods, innovations and skillful use of modern technology, the Second Lebanese War ended up as a struggle between direct and indirect strategies, with the unexpected success of the small state that relied on irregular means and strategies.

CHAPTER 9

SUMMARY AND A LOOK AHEAD

The years following the end of the Cold War's bipolar world order have led to a situation in which an ever-growing asymmetry has arisen in the military capabilities of many countries. Some major states, with greater ambitions and more economic power, have managed to gain remarkable advantages in conventional warfighting capabilities over smaller states. The weaker countries, to try to keep up with the large states, have continued to pursue the principle of "sameness" in the "competition in the arts and the instruments of force,"[526] and have responded by implementing one or a combination of the four traditional ways of forming a defense strategy. The analysis of these conventional warfare-focused frameworks in this project highlights several of their disadvantages. In the case of imitating major powers, small states trying to sustain large but uneconomical and

---

[526] Waltz, *Theory of International Politics*, 127.

obsolete military forces, were shown to be wasting resources and opportunities. These small states play right into the hands of their future adversaries by trying to fight on their adversaries' conventional terms. Alternatively, by joining alliances to overcome their conventional disadvantages, small countries become dependent on others for many facets of defense and continually run the risk of abandonment or entrapment by their allies. Neutrality, a third alternative, can be successful only if the enemy accepts and abides by that status. Finally, to acquire WMD may pay off well, but in the current international environment, its success seems highly unlikely, and even the smallest sign of the intention to develop such a capability can lead to much international pressure and perhaps disastrous results.

This thesis does not suggest that these methods never work for small states; however, this research intended to explore the possibility of another, more advantageous, way of homeland defense. By changing the focus from the idea of pursuing "sameness" to embracing "asymmetry," this project affirms the validity of establishing a professional irregular force and implementing an irregular strategy for the homeland defense of small states. The work was done on the assumption that an irregular approach could not only avoid the disadvantages of the four traditional frameworks, but provide a higher chance of success to a small state warring against a numerically and technologically superior enemy. Through longitudinal and cross-sectional analysis of six historical cases, including successful and failed irregular struggles, this project identified several key factors that make it reasonable for small states to consider such a strategy and build a professional irregular force.

One of the common characteristics that emerged from the cases presented in this thesis was that the technological and numerical advantages of the large states were overwhelming and the small states either lacked sufficient force to fight on the enemies' terms or they had already been defeated in conventional battle by their stronger foes. The recognition of enemy strength in conventional warfighting capabilities and the small states` limitations led to the implementation of irregular defensive strategies in all cases. While in the first four cases this approach arose from necessity during the war, in the last two cases the irregular strategy was formed long before the conflicts started. As the analysis demonstrated, the earlier a small state decided to implement an irregular strategy, the less pain it had to endure in building a substantial force and the supporting infrastructure for waging an irregular war. Generals Greene and von Lettow used their conventional forces to wage an irregular war. Though their soldiers had limited irregular-warfare experience, they had been trained for conventional war and their logistical system was designed to support such fighting, which was a serious disadvantage at the beginning of the wars. The Boers made a tragic mistake when they initially tried to employ their irregularly organized and trained forces in a conventional war. This was a

326

great example of the point that mastery at the tactical and operational levels in irregular warfare is paramount—but by itself insufficient to ensure final victory. It is necessary to have a clear, overarching irregular strategy that integrates and directs these lower-level capabilities and directs them toward the common higher goals. The Yugoslav partisan movement was built on an underground political organization that initially did not have a strategy or military force. Tito formed his irregular approach and his force during the actual fighting. In the cases of both the Chechens and Hezbollah, there was an existing irregular strategy with sufficient irregular force and supporting infrastructure. This enabled both small states to fight unexpectedly successful defensive wars against two of the strongest militaries in the world. In sum, all the small states studied turned to irregular warfare sooner or later, but they paid a lower price and were more successful if they switched before the war. Beyond the proper timing of the implementation of an irregular strategy, this research reveals several additional conditions worth thinking about for small states considering such an approach.

First, the case analyses highlight the necessity of a firm and unified political will among the small country's leaders in favor of an irregular strategy and professional irregular defense force. Political unity is required because an irregular strategy is a nontraditional way of defending a country, and in the case of a war, this approach can mean the initial loss of territorial sovereignty, letting invaders into the country without fighting, and waging a protracted war with much suffering inflicted upon civilians. This reality might be hard to sell to politicians and civil society. The understanding and support of the population is crucial for the success of an irregular strategy. Those small states that had the ability to unify their populations, whether based on powerful notions of nationalism, as in the case of the Americans, Yugoslavs, and Chechens, or on religion-based bonds like Hezbollah's, have the highest chance of successfully employing an irregular strategy against a superior enemy. As the analyzed conflicts demonstrate, if the population does not accept the invaders` rule and resists in every possible way while the small state`s forces launch irregular operations on a continuous basis against the invaders, the situation becomes close to impossible for the large state to sustain its control over the occupied territories.

Second, to implement an irregular warfare strategy successfully, there must be capable and willing military leaders from the highest to lowest levels who understand and accept the necessary changes in the existing conventional force structure, training system, and military culture as a whole. As the research shows, pre-conflict military training increases the effectiveness of every individual soldier and unit and also creates significant bias toward the conventional military culture in which they were raised. In all cases, it took unique individuals and unconventional thinking to pursue irregular strategies. The irregular-minded leaders studied had to fight their conventional-minded peers continually to implement their ideas. To avoid such conflict, small states considering an irregular strategy must conduct a drastic reorganization of their forces, including the firing of hard-core conventional leaders and replacement with open-minded commanders at all levels. Small states also have to create a training and education system that, while keeping some aspects of conventional warfare training, focuses on irregular warfare methods, especially on the essence of swarming.

Third, rough natural physical terrain and severe weather conditions have been crucial factors in waging many irregular wars, and those countries having such features were at an advantage, since these features by themselves could take away many conventional military advantages. However, those small states with fewer mountains and less wilderness can still consider implementing irregular warfare strategies. The Chechen and Lebanese cases provide supporting evidence of this. Though the physical terrain and weather played a key role in these cases, they also showed that with proper pre-conflict preparation and effective integration into the overall strategy, manmade features can be as important as natural ones. Most of today's countries experience a continuous growth of urban areas, which provides more advantageous terrain for them against conventional forces than they could imagine. Those small states with extended urban areas can create the most difficult battlefield for conventional attackers and the most advantageous for irregular defenders, through proper infrastructure preparation.

Fourth, as a paramount condition of a successful irregular defense strategy for small states, the analyzed cases highlight the importance of self-reliance and self-sustainment. Besides Hezbollah, all small states studied here fought against their conventional enemies without any significant outside support. The irregulars were successful by living off the land individually or in small units, and by creating an effective support system during the conflict, or building one before the war. While the large conventional formations required large amounts of resupply, the small irregular units could sustain themselves from small rations. The issue of self-sustainment was a crucial problem for both sides in every conflict, but since long and exposed supply lines are very vulnerable, they became a decisive disadvantage for the conventional side. Based on this understanding, any small state considering the implementation of an irregular strategy should be able to wage a war without significant outside support. The preparation of supporting infrastructure, including hideouts, hospitals, hidden approach routes, tunnel and bunker systems, weapon and ammunition caches etc., can be crucial to the successful conduct of an irregular war.

Finally, this research revealed the importance of knowing the enemy as much as possible while protecting the irregular force's own information from discovery. In the presented cases, the irregular fighters capitalized on their extensive knowledge of the enemy. For example, Francis Marion, Aslan Maskhadov, Tito, and several of their small-unit leaders had all previously served in the military forces of their future enemies. That service gave them detailed knowledge of their enemies' operational methods and the capabilities and limitations of their weapon systems. Similarly, the Boers and Hezbollah had knowledge of their adversaries through previous conflicts with them and made efforts to capitalize on the lessons from those earlier engagements. This kind of knowledge can be built easily today as well, since every country follows almost the same general principles of traditional war and their conventional military doctrine is widely available for study on the Internet. This could be one more reason for considering the introduction of an irregular defensive strategy. It would provide a significant advantage over highly predictable conventional units, since there is no such thing as an irregular doctrine or a common list of irregular warfare methods, which provides a unique unpredictability for irregular forces. The effectiveness of this element can be further increased by strict control and protection of information regarding the irregular strategy. The Chechens' kinship-based, network-type social relations, or the closed character of Lebanese society, seem to be the best frameworks for information security. Those small states with similar conditions could add one more force multiplier to their irregular strategy if they were to implement such an approach.

Although this summary suggests a strong motivation for small states to consider creating a professional, irregular defense force and homeland-defense strategy, the conduct of country-specific research in the following topics would further emphasize the utility of the proposed theory:

1. Is a professional irregular defense force cheaper than a conventional military, or not?

2. What size professional, irregular defense force could be sustained from the same budget used by the current conventional military?

3. Can a small state combine any of the four traditional defense frameworks in conjunction with a professional, irregular defense force and an irregular defense strategy?

4. How should a professional, irregular defense force be organized, trained, equipped, and sustained?

5. How long would it take to transform an existing conventional military culture and organization into a professional, irregular defense force?

Considering the differences among countries concerning their military capabilities, it is clear that in case of invasion, many small states will not be able to resist by means of conventional warfare. Even though, irregular warfare is as old as man and has been present in every conflict since the beginning of war, it has never been considered a state-level, grand strategy to win a war. Even the United States, the most powerful conventional military power, does not consider it a valid possibility. As John Arquilla notes in his book, *Insurgents, Raiders and Bandits: How Masters of Irregular Warfare Have Shaped Our World*, a Pentagon document issued in 2007 on irregular warfare still "reflects a curious lack of attention to the idea that irregular warfare may be employed by a standing military in a general conflict."[527] The geostrategic environment of today might be the setting in which to change this view. History teaches that those small states that are searching for self-reliant, effective homeland defense should stop pursuing the "sameness" path that leads to certain defeat. Instead they should innovate by starting to "harvest from the edges of strategic thought"[528]

[527] John Arquilla, *Insurgents, Raiders and Bandits: How Masters of Irregular Warfare Have Shaped Our World* (Maryland: The Rowman and Littlefield Publishing Group Inc, 2011), 7.

[528] John Arquilla, (2011) *Course lectures on Warfare in the Information Age,* DA Department, NPS.

particularly thought about irregular warfare— to enhance their prospects for successful self-defense and national survival.

LIST OF REFERENCES

Alexander, John K. *Samuel Adams: America's Revolutionary Politician*. Lanham: Rowman & Littlefield, 2002.

Arquilla, John (2011) *Course lectures on Warfare in the Information Age.* DA Department, NPS.

Arquilla, John and David Ronfeldt. *Swarming & the Future of Conflict*. Santa Monica: RAND Coorporation, 2000.

Arquilla John. *From Troy to Entebbe. Special Operations in Ancient and Modern Times.* University Press of America, 1996.

Arquilla, John. *Insurgents, Raiders and Bandits: How Masters of Irregular Warfare Have Shaped Our World.* Maryland: The Rowman and Littlefield Publishing Group Inc, 2011.

Arquilla, John and Theodore Karasik. "Chechnya: A Glimpse of Future Conflict." *Studies in Conflict and Terrorism*, Volume 22, Number 3, July 1, 1999, 217, accessed March 05, 2012, http://www.ingentaconnect.com/content/routledg/uter/1999/00 000022/00000003/art00003.

Arreguín-Toft, Ivan. *How the weak win wars: The Theory of Asymetric Conflict*. New York: Cambridge University Press, 2005.

Bagot, Elizabeth. "US Ambivalence and the Russo-Chechen Wars: Behind the Silence." *Stanford Journal of International Relations*, Volume XI Number. 1, 2009, 33. accessed March 09, 2012, http://www.stanford.edu/group/sjir/pdf/Chechnya_11.1.pdf.

Bergman, Ronen. *The Secret War with Iran*. New York: Free Press, 2008.

Biddle, Stephen and Jeffrey A. Friedman. *The 2006 Lebanon Campaign and the Future of the Warfare: Implications for Army and Defense Policy*. Carlisle: Strategic Studies Institute, 2008.

Cassidy, Robert M. *Russia in Afghanistan and Chechnya: Military Strategic Culture and the Paradoxes of Asymmetric Conflict*. Carlisle Barracks, PA: U.S. Army War College Strategic Studies Institute, 2003.

Celestan, Gregory J. Wounded Bear: The Ongoing Russian Military Operation in Chechnya. 1996, accessed February 29, 2012, http://fmso.leavenworth.army.mil/documents/wounded/wounded.htm#25.

Chaliand, Gérard. *Guerrilla Strategies. A Historical Anthology from the Long March to Afghanistan*. Berkley: University of California Press, 1982.

Che Guevara, Ernesto. *Guerrilla Warfare*. New York: Classic House Books, 2009.

Chivers, C. J. and Thom Shanker, "Georgia Eager to Rebuild its Defeated Armed Forces." The New York Times, 03, September, 2008, accessed October 03, 2011, http://www.nytimes.com/2008/09/03/world/europe/03georgia.html?pagewanted=print.

Clausewitz, Carl von. *On War*. Princeton: Princeton University Press, 1976.

Cloud, David S. "U.S. Speeds Up Bomb Delivery for Israelis." *New York Times*, 22 July 2006, accessed March 28, 2012, http://www.nytimes.com/2006/07/22/world/middleeast/22military.html?pagewanted=all.

Cobban, Helena. *The Making of Modern Lebanon*. Boulder:

Westview Press, 1985.
Cordesman, Anthony H. *Lessons of the 2006 Israeli-Hezbollah War*. Washington D. C.: Center for Strategic and International Studies, 2007.

Crooke, Alastair and Mark Perry. "How Hezbollah Defeated Israel, Part 1: Winning the intelligence war." *Asia Times*, 12 Octorber 2006, accessed March 25, 2012, http://www.atimes.com/atimes/Middle_East/HJ12Ak01.html.

Deakin, Frederick William. *The Embattled Mountain*. London: Oxford University Press, 1971.

De Wet, Christiaan Rudolf. *Three Years War*. New York: Charles Scribner's Son, 1985.

Doyle, Sir Arthur Conan. *The Great Boer War*. New York: McClure Phillips and Company, 1902.

Dunlop, John Boyd. *Russia Confronts Chechnya: Roots of a Separatist Conflict*. Cambridge: Cambridge University Press, 1998.

Eben, Kaplan, "Profile: Hassan Nasrallah," Council on Foreign Relations, July 20, 2006, accessed March 25, 2012, http://www.cfr.org/publication/11132/profile.html.

Exum, Andrew. *Hizballah at War. A Military Assessment*. Washington D.C.: Washington Institute for Near East Policy, 2006.

Farquhar, Scott C. *"Back to Basics, A Study of the Second Lebanon War and Operation Cast Lead."* (Fort Leavenworth, Kansas Combat Studies Institute Press, 2009): 1-156.

Farwell, Byron. *The Great War in Africa, 1914–1918*. New York: W.W. Norton & Company, 1989.

Farwell, Byron. *The Great Boer War*. New York: Penguin, 1976.

Fast, Howard. *Tito and his People*. Winnipeg: Contemporary Publishers, 1944.

Faurby, Ib and Marta-Lisa Magnusson. "The Battle(s) of Grozny." *Baltic Defense Review*, 2/1999, 77, accessed March 06, 2012,
http://www.bdcol.ee/files/docs/bdreview/07bdr299.pdf.

Felix, Christopher. *A Short Course in the Secret War*. New York: Madison Books, 2001.

"Francis Marion." Encyclopedia of World Biography. 2004. *Encyclopedia.com*. accessed August 25, 2011,
http://www.encyclopedia.com/doc/1G2-3404704217.html.

Freedman, Lawrence. *Deterrence*. New York: Polity Press, 2004.

Fulghum, David. "Doubt as a Weapon." *Aviation Week & Space Technology*," 27 November 2006.

Gall, Carlotta and Thomas de Waal. *Chechnya: Calamity in the Caucasus*. London: New York University Press, 1998.

Gann, Lewis H. *Guerrillas in History*. Stanford, CA: Hoover Institution Press, 1971.

Gardner, Brian. *German East. The Story of the First World War in East Africa*. London: Cassell and Company ltd., 1963.

German Antiguerrilla Operations in the Balkans. 1941-1944. Washington D.C.: Department of the Army, 1954, accessed January 09, 2012,
http://cgsc.cdmhost.com/cdm/singleitem/collection/p4013coll8/id/2459.

Giap, Vo Nguyen. *The Military Art of People's War Selected Writings of General Vo Nguyen Giap*. edited by Russel Stetler. Monthly Review Press, 1970.

Grant, Maurice Harold, *History of the War in South Africa*. London: Hurst and Blackett Limited, 1907.

Hahlweg, Werner. "Clausewitz and Guerrilla Warfare." *Journal of Strategic Studies* 9 (1986): 127-132.

Hamzeh, Nizar A. "Lebanon's Hizbullah: from Islamic Revolution to Parliamentary Accommodation." *Third World Quarterly*, Volume 14, Number 2, 1993, accessed March 22, 2012, http://ddc.aub.edu.lb/projects/pspa/hamzeh2.html.

Handel, Michael I. *Weak States in the International System*. Gainsborough: Frank Cass and Co Ltd, 1990.

Harik, Judith Palmer. *Hezbollah: The Changing Face of Terrorism*. New York: I. B. Tauris, 2004.

Henze, Paul Bernard. *Islam in the North Caucasus.* Santa Monica: RAND Corporation, 1995.

Higginbotham, Don *The War of American Independence: Military Attitudes, Policies, and Practice, 1763–1789*. Northeastern University Press, 1983.

Huth, Paul K. "Deterrence and International Conflict: Empirical Findings and Theoretical Debate." *Annual Review of Political Science* 2 (1999): 25-48.

Irregular warfare (IW) Joint Operating Concept (JOC), Version 1, Department of Defense, 2007.
James, William Dobein. *Swamp Fox: General Francis Marion and his Irregular Fighters of the American Revolutionary War.* St Petersburg: Red and Black Publishers, 2010.

Joes, Anthony James. *America and Guerrilla Warfare.* Lexington: The University Press of Kentucky, 2000.

Joes, Anthony James. *Guerrilla Warfare. A Historical,*

Biographical, and Bibliographical Sourcebook. Westport:
Greenwood Press, 1996.

Johnson, David E."Minding the Middle: Insights from
Hezbollah and Hamas for
Future Warfare," *Strategic Insights*, Volume 10, Special Issue,
October 2011, 125. accessed March 22, 2012,
http://www.nps.edu/Academics/Centers/CCC/Research-
Publications/StrategicInsights/2011/Oct/SI-v10-FoW_pg124-
137_Johnson.pdf.

Johnson, Joshua. "From Cuba to Bolivia: Guevara's Foco
Theory in Practice." *Innovations: a Journal of Politics*,
Volume 6 (2006): 27.

Johnston, Paul. "Doctrine is not enough: The Effect of
Doctrine on the Behavior of Armies." *Parameters*: US Army
War College Quarterly, 2000.

Jordan Nicole. The *Popular Front and Central Europe. The
Dilemmas of French Impotence 1918-1940*. New York:
Cambridge University Press, 1992.

Judd, Denis and Keith Surridge. *The Boer War.* New York:
Palgrave MacMillan, 2003.

Kalb, Marvin. "The Israeli-Hezbollah War of 2006: The
Media As a Weapon in Asymmetrical
Conflict." *Joan Shorenstein Center on the Press, Politics and
Public Policy*, February 2007, 4, accessed March 25,
2012,http://www.ksg.harvard.edu/presspol/research_publicatio
ns/papers/research_papers/R29.pdf.

Karasik, Theodore. "Chechen Clan Tactics and Russian
Warfare." CACI Analyst, 15 March 2000, accessed March 05,
2012, http://cacianalyst.org/?q=node/353

Karsh, Efraim. *Neutrality and Small States*. Worcester: Billing
and Sons Ltd, 1988.

Kassimeris, Christos. "Greek Response to the Cyprus Invasion" *Small Wars and Insurgencies* 19, number 2. (2008): 256–273, accessed November 01, 2011, http://www.tandfonline.com/doi/abs/10.1080/0959231080206 1398?journalCode=fswi20#preview.

Ketchum, Richard M. *Saratoga: Turning Point of America's Revolutionary War*. Henry Holt, 1997.

Knezys, Stasys and Romanas Sedlickas. *The War in Chechnya*. College Station: Texas A and M University, 1999.

Kwasny, Mark V. *Washington's Partisan War, 1775–1783*. Ohio: Kent, 1996.

Labaree, Benjamin W. *The Boston Tea Party*. Boston: Northeastern University Press, 1979.

Laqueur, Walter. *Guerrilla Warfare. A Historical and Critical Study*. New Brunswick: Transaction Publishers, 1998.

Lettow-Vorbeck, Paul Emil Von, *My Reminiscences of East Africa*, Uckfield: The Naval and Military Press ltd.

Liddell Hart, Basil H. *Strategy, The Indirect Approach*. Natraj Publisher, 2003.

Mack, Andrew. "Why Big Nations Lose Small Wars." *Word Politics*, Volume: 27, Issue: 2, (1975): 176.

Mahan, Alfred Thayer. *The Story of the War in South Africa*. London: William Clowes, 1900.

McCormick, Gordon H. (2011) *Seminar on Guerrilla Warfare*. DA Department, NPS.

McRaven, William H. *Spec Ops, Case Studies in Special Operations Warfare: Theory and Practice*. San Marin: Presidio Press, 1995.

Miller, Charles. *Battle for the Bundu: The First World War in East Africa*. New York: MacMillan Publishing Co., Inc. 1974.

Oliker, Olga. *Russia's Chechen Wars 1994-2000: Lessons from Urban Combat*. Santa Monica: Rand Corporation, 2001.

Paice, Edward. *Tip and Run. The Untold Tragedy of the Great War in Africa*. London: Phoenix, 2008.

Pakenham, Thomas. *The Boer War*. New York: Random House, 1979.

Prichard, Harry Lionel. *History of the Royal Corps of Engineers, Vol. VII*. Chatham: The Institute of Royal Engineers, 1952.

Ratcliffe, Alexander. *Partisan Warfare. A Treatise Based on Combat Experiences in the Balkans*. Munich: Historical Division Headquarters US Army, Europe,1953.

Reiter, Erich and Heinz Gaertner. *Small States and Alliances*. VIENNA: Physica-Verlag, 2001.

Reitz, Deneys and J. C. Smuts, *Commando: A Boer Journal of the Boer War*, London: Faber and Faber Limited, 1929.

Richardson, Michael. (2011) *Course lectures on Deterrence, Coercion and Crisis Management.* DA Department, NPS.

Rothstein, Robert L. *Alliances and Small Powers*. Columbia University Press, 1968.

Schelling, Thomas C. *Arms and Influence*. New Haven: Yale University Press, 1966.

Seely, Robert. *Russo-Chechen Conflict, 1800-2000. A Deadly Embrace*. New York: Frank Cass Publishers, 2004.

Seidner, Stanley S. *Marshal Edward Śmigły-Rydz and the Defense of Poland.* New York: Michigan University Press,

1978.

Shirer, William L. *The Rise and Fall of the Third Reich: A History of Nazi Germany*. New York: Simon and Schuster, 1990.

Smith, Bradley F. and Agnes Peterson. *Heinrich Himmler Geheimreden 1933 bis 1945*. Propyläen Verlag, 1974.

Smith, Iain R. *The Origins of the South African War 1890-1902*. Essex: Longman Group Limited, 1996.

Smuts, Jan. *Memoirs of the Boer War*. London: Jonathan Ball Publishers, 1997.

Strachan, Hew and Andreas Herberg-Rothe. *Clausewitz in the Twenty First Century*. Oxford: Oxford University Press, 2007.

Summers Jr, Harry G. *On Strategy: a Critical Analysis of the Vietnam War*. Novato: Presidio Press, 1982

The ROK-US Mutual DefenseTreaty, accessed November 01, 2011, http://www.koreaembassyusa.org/bilateral/military/eng_military4.asp.

Thomas, Timothy L. "The Caucasus conflict and Russian security: The Russian armed forces confront Chechnya III. The battle for Grozny, 1–26 January 1995." *The Journal of Slavic Military Studies,* Volume 10 Issue 1, 1997, 69, accessed March 09, 2012, http://www.tandfonline.com/doi/pdf/10.1080/13518049708430276.

Thucydides. *History of the Peloponnesian War*. translated by Rex Warner. New York: Penguin Group, 1972.

Tira, Ron. "Breaking the Amoeba's Bones." *Strategic Assessment*, Jaffee Center for Strategic Studies, Tel Aviv University, Vol. 9, No.

3, November 2006, 9, accessed March 24, 2012,
http://www.inss.org.il/publications.php?cat=21&incat=&read=84.

Trenin, Dimitri V. and Aleksei V. Malashenko. *Russia's Relentless Frontier: The Chechnya Factor in Post-Soviet Russia.* Washington, DC: Carnegie Endowment for International Peace, 2008.

Tse-tung, Mao. *On Guerrilla Warfare* translated by Samuel B. Griffith. Urbana:University of Illinois Press, 2000.

United States Information Pertaining to the Treaty on the Non-Proliferation of Nuclear Weapons, 2010, 2-7. accessed October 06, 2011,
http://www.state.gov/documents/organization/141928.pdf.

U.S. Congress, Office of "Technology Assessment, *Proliferation of Weapons of Mass Destruction: Assessing the Rish, OTA-ISC-559* Washington, DC: U.S. Government Printing Office, August 1993.

Van Creveld, Martin. *The Transformation of War*, New York: The Free Press, 1991.

Walt, Stephen. *The Origins of Alliances.* Ithaca: Cornell University Press, 1987.

Waltz, Kenneth N. *Theory of International Politics.* New York: McGraw-Hill, 1979.

Waltzer, Michael. *Just and Unjust Wars. A Moral Argument with Historical Illustration.* New York: Basic Books, 2000.

Weller, Jac "Irregular but Effective: Partisan Weapons Tactics in the American Revolution: Southern Theatre." *Military Affairs.* (Fall 1967).

Wessels, André. "Boer Guerrilla and British Counter-guerrilla Operations in South Africa 1899 to 1902."

Scientia Militaria: South African Journal of Military Studies 39 (2011).

Wiberg, Hakan. "The Security of Small Nations: Challenges and Defences." *Journal of Peace Research,* Volume 24 Number 4 (1987): 339-350.

Wight, Martin. *Power Politics*. Penguin Books Ltd, 1979.

Williams, Rocky. "South African Guerrilla Armies. The Impact of Guerrilla Armies on the Creation of South Africa's Armed Forces." Monograph 127 (2006), accessed November 28, 2011, http://www.iss.co.za/pgcontent.php?UID=18440.

Wisser, John P. *The Second Boer War. 1899-1900*. Kansas: Hudson-Kimberly Publishing Company, 1901.

Wright, Lawrence. *The Looming Tower: Al-Qaeda and the Road to 9/11*. New York: Vintage Books, 2006.

Zobel, Hiller B. *The Boston Massacre*. New York: W.W. Norton & Company, 1970